"In *Beautiful Bodies*, lifel[ong...] amines the evolution of t[...] of divine justice, love, an[d...] nity—particularly the community of the church. For any readers troubled by seeing Augustine as body-hating or curmudgeonly, Miles evokes, interrogates, renovates, and restores for us that generous-minded ancient intelligence that has had such an abiding influence on Christians in a deeply appreciative and invigorating way."

—**Jennifer M. Phillips**, former rector, St. John's Episcopal Church Westwood

"Margaret Miles, who has had a long career bringing readers to new and deeper understanding of Augustine, offers in this book an opportunity to think and feel with Augustine as he grew and changed from his youth to old age. Dealing with a number of tensions in his thought, Miles persuades the reader to tangle with the issues not to get a systematic answer but to live into the way Augustine grappled with them as an embodied and thoughtful theologian and philosopher."

—**Jennifer Hockenbery**, dean of humanities, St. Norbert College

"In this nuanced and deeply felt meditation on the aging Augustine, Margaret Miles lifts up an Augustine attuned from his own life experience to the miraculous wonder of the everyday: from sky, earth, air, and waters, to human being itself. *Beautiful Bodies* draws on a half century of Miles's passionate reading, struggling, thinking, and feeling with Augustine to offer her own readers an aching model for living fully in the beauty of the now and opening oneself to future transformations."

—**Ann Pellegrini**, professor of performance studies & social and cultural analysis, New York University

"Scholars often draw contrasts between Augustine's early and later thought, but no one does so with such insight and sensitivity as Margaret Miles in this book. Miles tracks gentle shifts of attitude, conviction, and emotion in the acutely self-aware North African bishop, who, during the late autumn of his life, amended and sometimes revised his beliefs, attitudes, and perspectives on questions enthralling him since his youth. This is a gorgeous study of, arguably, the most impactful personality of late antiquity."

—**Christopher Ocker**, professor of the history of Christianity, San Francisco Theological Seminary

"It is difficult to think of any theologian who has devoted such engaged reflection and pellucid insight into 'body' across the centuries. Margaret Miles's most recent book on Augustine reveals how she has developed a new sort of hermeneutic: her own embodiment as insight into historical bodies."

—**Martin Laird**, OSA, professor of early Christian studies, Villanova University

Beautiful Bodies

Beautiful Bodies

Augustine, nunc et tunc

Margaret R. Miles

CASCADE *Books* • Eugene, Oregon

BEAUTIFUL BODIES
Augustine, nunc et tunc

Copyright © 2024 Margaret R. Miles. All rights reserved. Except for brief quotations in critical publications or reviews, no part of this book may be reproduced in any manner without prior written permission from the publisher. Write: Permissions, Wipf and Stock Publishers, 199 W. 8th Ave., Suite 3, Eugene, OR 97401.

Cascade Books
An Imprint of Wipf and Stock Publishers
199 W. 8th Ave., Suite 3
Eugene, OR 97401

www.wipfandstock.com

PAPERBACK ISBN: 978-1-6667-6730-8
HARDCOVER ISBN: 978-1-6667-6731-5
EBOOK ISBN: 978-1-6667-6732-2

Cataloguing-in-Publication data:

Names: Miles, Margaret R., author.

Title: Beautiful bodies : Augustine, nunc et tunc / Margaret R. Miles.

Description: Eugene, OR : Cascade Books, 2024 | **Includes bibliographical references and index.**

Identifiers: ISBN 978-1-6667-6730-8 (paperback) | ISBN 978-1-6667-6731-5 (hardcover) | ISBN 978-1-6667-6732-2 (ebook)

Subjects: LCSH: Augustine,-of Hippo, Saint,–354–430. | Augustine, of Hippo, Saint, 354–430—Ontology. | Human body—Religious aspects—Christianity.

Classification: BT701 .M53 2024 (paperback) | BT701 .M53 (ebook)

VERSION NUMBER 05/22/24

For The Reverend Massey Shepherd, PhD, my first teacher of Augustine of Hippo.

Professor Shepherd also taught me Latin. When I began doctoral studies in 1974 at the Graduate Theological Union, I was teaching at a community college in Sonora, California, and commuting three hours each way twice a week to classes in Berkeley, memorizing Latin vocabulary all the way. Since I could not take a five-day-a-week Latin course, "Shep" (as he was affectionately known to colleagues and students) offered most generously to teach me Latin in an independent study. His magnanimous offer (plus a parking place at the Church Divinity School of the Pacific), made doctoral studies possible for me. Lacking either, the difficulties may have been too great.

Professor Shepherd insisted that Augustine must be heard in his own language, a truth that I came to appreciate many times by comparing the Latin text with translations. He was not content simply to correct me as I laboriously picked my way through Augustine's beautiful Latin. In each of our sessions he also read aloud a paragraph or two from a sermon of Augustine's to give me a feeling of the *music* of the language, to help me to hear that, beyond my struggle to memorize vocabulary and verb paradigms, Augustine sings—in Latin! I am immensely grateful to have begun my study of St. Augustine with someone who loved Augustine's writings. Professor Shepherd's delight was communicable and enduring. I feel it to this day.

February 15, 2023
Berkeley, California

Is not our absorbing love of life really soul's love for its body, a body which will haunt it until that body is returned to it risen and glorious?

—*De genesi ad litteram* 12.35.68

Contents

Preface | ix
Acknowledgments | xiii
Abbreviations | xv
Introduction: Augustine, Old | xvii

Chapter One
The Inner Eye of the Beholder: St. Augustine on Miracles | 1

Chapter Two
St. Augustine's Last Desire | 18

Centerpiece
Breathing Together | 46

Chapter Three
How St. Augustine Could Love the God in Whom He Believed | 53

Chapter Four
St. Augustine's Tears: Recollecting and Reconsidering a Life | 74

Chapter Five
Resurrected Bodies | 97

Translations Cited | 113
Bibliography | 117
Index | 121

Preface

This flesh will rise, this flesh which is buried, which dies, which is perceived, which is touched.

(*S.* 264.4)

IN ABOUT 1500 CE, the Italian artist Luca Signorelli translated Augustine's description of resurrected bodies in *The City of God* (*De ciuitate dei*) to painted figures. Signorelli's *Resurrection of the Flesh* in the San Brizio Chapel, Orvieto Cathedral, pictures trumpeting angels announcing the resurrection, as fleshed and muscled bodies climb out of graves, *pulled by their eyes*.[1] Skulls and bones lie discarded, or are incorporated into risen bodies. The naked figures appear to exult in their weightlessness, stretching into the air, or they assist others who are emerging from graves. Groups of the newly resurrected stroll "without a trace of clumsiness."[2] No blemishes or deformities are visible.[3] They talk or gaze silently at

---

1. *Ciu.* 22.29: "It is indeed most probable that we shall then see the physical bodies of the new heaven and the new earth in such a fashion as to observe God in utter clarity and distinctness, seeing him present everywhere and governing the whole material world by means of the bodies we will see wherever we turn our eyes."

2. *Ciu.* 13.24.

3. *Ench.* 91: "The bodies of the saints shall rise again free from any defect,

one another's beauty; women and men embrace gently, without urgency.[4] All appear to be young adults.[5] They are neither fat nor thin.[6] In the foreground, a muscular young man poses; sporting the long hair of Renaissance fashion, he is the epitome of male beauty.[7] There are *no shadows* in Signorelli's painting; Augustine cited the "brightness" of Jesus's resurrected body as an indication that in the day of resurrection, "the just shall shine forth as the sun in the kingdom of their father" (Matt 13:43). These resurrected bodies are free from the mortality that previously marred that "frailer loveliness of flesh and blood."[8]

For Augustine, human bodies are the most compelling example of God's power to bring something from nothing. He devoted the final chapters of *The City of God* to a detailed description of the beauty of *present* bodies, Christians' strongest, most intimate *connection* to the beauty of resurrected bodies. Until Augustine saw present bodies as beautiful, he could not imagine resurrected bodies in "living color." As an old man, he saw human bodies (*nunc*) as beautiful creations of the Creator who *is* beauty.[9] The ability to see present bodies as beautiful in their marvelous intricacy facilitates belief in resurrected bodies recreated *as* beauty. According to Augustine, resurrected bodies *are* the bodies of human experience, lacking only the marring stigma of mortality:

> *If now* in such frailty of the flesh and in such weak operation of our members, such great beauty of body appears that it entices the passionate and stimulates the learned to investigate it . . . how much more beautiful will the

---

from every blemish, as from all corruption, weight, and impediment. . . . Their ease of movement shall be as complete as their happiness."

4. *Ciu.* 22.27: "We shall enjoy each other's beauty without any lust."

5. *Ciu.* 22.15: Resurrected bodies will be "neither older nor younger than Christ," thus about thirty years old.

6. *Ciu.* 22.19.

7. *Ciu.* 19.19: "dress or manner of life . . . does not matter to the heavenly city."

8. Plato, *Symposium* 211c–e.

9. *Conf.* 10.6.

body be then where there will be no passion, no miserable necessity, but instead unending eternity, beautiful truth, and the utmost happiness.[10]

---

10. S. 243.8.

Acknowledgments

WITH GREAT APPRECIATION I thank the longtime editor of my books, Charlie Collier, at Cascade Books, Wipf and Stock Publishers. Charlie has welcomed my manuscripts with enthusiasm for over fifteen years. He never believed me when I told him that the current manuscript was to be my last. He reminded me gently that he had heard that threat—or promise—several times before. But now I am eighty-six years old, and this book *is* my swan song to an author I have studied with fascination, perplexity, excitement, admiration, and love for over fifty years.

Many thanks to friends at the Augustinian Institute, Villanova University, who encouraged my recent love for the old Augustine, rich with the experience of a life passionately and thoughtfully lived. I thank especially Professor Martin Laird, OSA, and Professor James Wetzel, director of the Institute. During the COVID-19 pandemic, library research was more difficult than usual. The Flora Lamson Hewlett Library of the Graduate Theological Union in Berkeley, California, like other responsible libraries, restricted entrance for many months, but books could be requested. Research Librarian Naw San KD was the most frequent provider of my Latin volumes. Lacking his skill and good cheer, my research would have been much more difficult. Thank you!

I thank Professor Ian Clausen, editor of *Augustinian Studies*, who graciously granted permission to publish slightly altered versions of three of my articles published in the journal.

Acknowledgments

"St. Augustine's Tears: Recollecting and Reconsidering a Life." *AS* 51:2 (2020) 155–76.

"St. Augustine's Last Desire." *AS* 52:2 (2021) 135–60.

"How St. Augustine Could Love the God in Whom He Believed." *AS* 54:1 (2023) 23–42.

Parts of "Sex and the City (of God): Is Sex Forfeited or Fulfilled in Augustine's Resurrection of Body?" *Journal of the American Academy of Religion* 73:2 (2005) 307–27, are included in chapter 5, "Resurrected Bodies."

Alterations of previously published articles were made primarily to render the text accessible to non-Latin readers.

Abbreviations

Ad Simplicianum	*simpl.*
Confessiones	*conf.*
Contra Iulianum	*c. Iul.*
Contra Iulianum opus imperfectum	*c. Iul. opus imperf.*
De beata uita	*beata u.*
De bono coniugali	*b. coniug.*
De catechizandis rudibus	*cat. rud.*
De ciuitate dei	*ciu.*
De correptione et gratia	*corrept.*
De doctrina christiana	*doct. chr.*
De dono perseuerantiae	*perseu.*
De fide et symbol	*f. et sym.*
De genesi ad litteram	*Gn. litt*
De musica	*mus.*
De natura et gratia	*nat. et grat.*
De nuptiis et concupiscentia	*nupt. et conc.*
De octo Dulcitii questionibus	*Dulc. qu.*
De praedestinationes sanctorum	*praed. sanct.*

Abbreviations

De quantitate animae	*an. quant.*
De sancta uirginitate	*uirg.*
De spiritu et littera	*spir. et litt.*
De trinitate	*trin.*
De uera religione	*uera. rel.*
De utilitate credendi	*util. cred.*
Enchiridion	*ench.*
Enarrationes in Psalmos	*en. ps.*
Epistulae	*ep.*
In epistulam Ioannis ad Parthos tract.	*ep. Io. tr.*
In Iohannis euangelium tractatus	*Io. eu. tr.*
Retractiones	*retr.*
Sermones	*s.*
Soliloquia	*Sol.*

Introduction
Augustine, Old

As a young man, Augustine had two arenas of urgent interest in bodies. First, his *Confessions* (*Confessiones*) describe his compulsive sexual interest—perhaps no more avid than that of any young man of his, or any, society—but nevertheless, deeply troubling to Augustine. Second, his education in the Platonic tradition had taught him that bodies must be "overlooked"—literally, "looked-over"—by one who seeks wisdom. Augustine was such a man. He recalled later that he was "on fire" to seek wisdom at the age of nineteen when he read Cicero's *Hortensius*.[1] Strong sexual urgency, together with an incandescent longing for wisdom, gripped him, struggling, in a vortex of powerful but seemingly incompatible desires. After decades of experience and thought, as an old man, Augustine recognized bodies, both present and future bodies, as integral to persons—and utterly *beautiful*.

Each of the chapters of this book explores a topic on which Augustine thought and spoke quite differently in old age than he did as a young man, or even in early middle age. As a proud young professor of rhetoric he had thought that Jesus's divinity was disastrously degraded by his human body, a view consistent with his Platonic education. One of the several conversions of his youth,

---

1. *Conf.* 3.4; in 53 BCE Cicero became a consul, the highest office in the Roman republic. He was a philosopher and public speaker, skilled in rhetoric, and known for his religious perspective; for example, he taught that the universe itself is God.

Introduction

described in his *Confessions*, was his conversion to the humility he discovered in the humble Jesus. Throughout his career as theologian, preacher, and teacher, Augustine advocated humility, *the posture in which learning is possible*. His early writings attempt to reconcile his Christian learning within the philosophical worldview he was taught as a youth; he found that he could not do so. Augustine's emerging esteem for human bodies is a measure of his distance from his Platonic education. Yet he was also committed to integrating, rather than summarily rejecting, whatever remained valuable to him from his secular education.[2]

The *method* of each of the chapters of this book silently argues what the text argues explicitly, namely, that Augustine cannot be assumed to hold one vantage point on a topic of importance throughout his Christian life. His old-age view of the status and value of bodies presumes *both* his formidable knowledge of Christian Scripture and his long experience as a pastor. Lacking attention to his age, current circumstances, immediate concerns (such as dissident interpretations of doctrine he considered heretical), and other relevant factors, claiming that "Augustine said" (that is, proof-texting) is not, or is not necessarily, decisive. Augustine's readers must always expect his lively mind to be in motion, seeking, evaluating possible interpretations, learning. In short, the method, as well as the content of these chapters, demonstrates that caution must be exercised in making categorical statements about Augustine's views on miracles (chapter 2), meditation (chapters 3 and 5), and God's activity in the inner self (Centerpiece and throughout).

Chapter 1: Augustine's view of the occurrence and value of miracles changed dramatically across an approximately forty-year period. As a young priest, he thought that miracles were necessary

---

2. An example is his regard for rhetoric: in early middle age when he wrote *conf.*, he dismissed his "professorship of lies" (*conf.* 9.2). Almost thirty years later, when he reconsidered the value of rhetoric as he wrote chapter 4 of *De doctrina christiana* (*doct. chr.*), c. 426, he argued that the skills of effective public speaking should not be left to "those who wish to urge falsehoods," while the defenders of truth, ignorant of rhetorical skills, do not "know how to make their listeners benevolent, or attentive, or docile," but whose address is "sluggish, cold, or somnolent. Who is so foolish as to think this to be wisdom?" (*doct. chr.* 2.3).

Introduction

in an early stage of Christianity in order to elicit belief "before anyone was fit to reason about divine and invisible things."[3] However, he wrote, miracles are no longer needed (because of the establishment of the Christian Church). Nevertheless, almost forty years later, he enthusiastically supported the authentication and publication of contemporary miracles, devoting large sections of the last chapters (written c. 425–27 CE) of *The City of God* to discussion of contemporary miracles.

In the chapters of this book, Augustine also explored the connection between miracles and the doctrine of the resurrection of bodies. He repeatedly addressed the Platonist Porphyry (d. 304 CE), whose vendetta against Christianity attacked the "ridiculous" idea that all human beings would be resurrected to immortal reward or punishment. He *felt deeply* the difficulty of belief, even for Christians, in this most "unbelievable" Christian doctrine. Augustine's about-face on miracles, articulated primarily in the sermons of his last decade, reveals an integration of his theology and his many years of pastoral experience.

Chapter 2 explores Augustine's practice of meditation, which, together with his study of Scripture, formed the nucleus of his Christian life, providing the sustenance with which he was nourished and with which he nourished his hearers. His early training in the art of rhetoric contributed to his conception of effective meditation as a series of carefully calibrated steps, but he described those steps quite differently at different times in his life.

Centerpiece introduces an important mid-life revision in Augustine's primary self-identity. His *Confessions,* written in early middle age, explored God's formative action *within* Augustine's own choices and the events and circumstances of his life. A fundamental transition in his understanding of *himself* is traceable in his fifth-century preaching on the Psalms.[4] Avoiding the danger of

---

3. *Uera. rel.* 25.47; trans. Burleigh, *St. Augustine.*

4. Grove, *Augustine on Memory;* this fine book documents a fundamental change in St. Augustine's perspective, which, until it was documented, was largely ignored; once alerted to it, however, it pops into the reader's eye everywhere in Augustine's later writings, especially in his sermons.

Introduction

being "stuck in the self," Augustine moved *from* a focus on the individual, "God and the soul," *to* a communally constructed identity as a member of the "body of Christ." His identity as member of "the whole Christ" is central to Augustine's later sermons and writings.

Chapter 3, "How St. Augustine Could Love the God in Whom He Believed," represents my effort to resolve an apparent dissonance—if not contradiction—I have struggled to understand for more than fifty years, that is, ever since I began to study Augustine. Augustine portrayed God as predestining individuals to an everlasting, nonnegotiable destiny of heaven or hell "before the foundation of the world," yet he also repeatedly and movingly described God as the embodiment and source of love, a God who "*first loved us*" (1 John 4:19), attracting human love in return. Augustine's fifth-century sermons indicate how he understood these seemingly opposing energies. In the words of Étienne Gilson, Augustine discovered that "it is eminently reasonable not to rely on reason alone."[5]

Yet, Augustine was a litigious defender of *doctrine*, especially those doctrines he defended near the end of his life, namely, original sin, predestination, and perseverance. Although he professed himself weary of doctrinal fisticuffs in old age, he did not simply reiterate his committed allegiance to these doctrines. Rather, he continued to debate opponents until he died; in fact, at his death, he left unfinished a treatise addressed to his last opponent, the exiled Pelagian Julian of Eclanum. Doctrine was undoubtedly critically important to Augustine. Chapter 4 describes my understanding of this disparity.

Chapter 4 is titled "Augustine's Tears: Reconstructing and Reconsidering a Life." Peter Brown, Augustine's twentieth-century biographer, concluded his account of the barbarian Vandals' assault on Hippo: "Augustine lived to see violence destroy his life's work in Africa."[6] Augustine died in the third month of the Vandals' fourteen-month siege of Hippo. Yet, despite the ultimate evacuation and destruction of Hippo, Possidius, Augustine's friend and

---

5. Gilson, *Christian Philosophy*, 227.
6. Brown, *Augustine*, 429.

Introduction

fifth-century biographer, catalogued Augustine's prodigious writings, which were preserved.[7] Possidius, who lived for many years in Augustine's monastery, described Augustine's last days, his requests and preoccupations as he approached death.[8] He admired both the quantity and the quality of Augustine's writings, but he wrote: "I think that those who gained most from him were those who had been able actually to see and hear him as he spoke in church."[9]

Chapter 5: Augustine was a lover of beauty, as is evident from his earliest writings. Recalling his lost early treatise "On the Beautiful and the Fitting," he asked, "Do we love anything but what is beautiful?" His *Confessions*, in which he called God "Beauty so old and so new,"[10] can be read as the beginning stages of a conversion to a beauty that he did not find in sex or worldly achievement.[11]

Although Augustine commented on the beauty of nature in early writings, he did not—until old age—discuss the physical beauty of human bodies as theologically significant. Significantly, even his detailed description of his youthful lust never suggested that his attraction was based on (or even was a part of) his appreciation of beauty.[12] Chapter 5, "Resurrected Bodies," concludes with Augustine's last discussion of the beauty of human bodies, *both* present bodies and resurrection bodies. His use of the syncrisis,

---

7. Brown, *Augustine*, 436–37; Vandals were Arian Christians, but this fact does not seem to explain the preservation of Augustine's library, as Vandals had tortured to death two Catholic bishops in towns they captured in 429 CE.

8. Possidius's account is discussed in chapter 5.

9. Possidius, *Uita* 31.9.

10. *Conf.* 3.6.

11. Later, in his sermons on the First Epistle of John, he quoted 1 John 4:16, "God is love," commenting that no higher commendation can be given than "to say that God is love" (*ep. Io. tr.* 7.4); the same can be said of naming God "beauty so old and so new." Augustine called only one other entity "God," namely, "life itself" (*doct. chr.* 1.8).

12. I venture the undocumented suggestion that St. Augustine is likely to have found the conventionally designated objects of possessive lust of his own (or any) society a barrier to recognizing beauty. An appreciation of beauty requires a kind of spiritual vision that is effectively blocked by acquisitive lust. His last discussion of beauty (*ciu.* 22.21) insisted on physical beauty as fundamentally non-separable from the beauty of the whole person.

Introduction

nunc et tunc, emphasizes both the distinctness and the continuity of human bodies.[13] This continuity became the basis of his urgent pastoral project, namely, to help his beloved companions in the Body of Christ to believe in the resurrection of bodies.

THEMES

Two major themes recur across chapters in this volume. The first focuses on Augustine's understanding of the central importance of *feeling*. Among intellectuals in Augustine's society, and certainly in twenty-first-century (post-Cartesian) academia, feeling was/is considered inessential, even an obstacle, to clear thinking. Yet Augustine learned, "by [his] own experience,"[14] that *will* (*uolantas*), strongly advocated by mind but not supported by feeling, cannot act. His preamble to the narrative of his conversion to celibacy, in *conf*. 8, explicitly and repeatedly denies that he needed mental clarity before he could commit to God's service. It was his strongly conflicting *feelings* that required resolution.

Later, as a preacher, Augustine did not seek to reason with his hearers, but rather to transmit the *feeling* that was the substance, the inner meaning, of his words. But the communication of feeling, no matter how skillful, is not something the preacher can *do to* passive hearers. To be effective, the preacher's feeling must engage *active* listeners who will hear "in the heart." *Both* preaching *and* hearing *intus* are necessary if a communication of feeling is to occur. Augustine's readers encounter an even greater difficulty than hearing Augustine's living voice in the heart; we must endeavor to hear Augustine's sermons "in the heart" through words on the page.

To understand Augustine, his readers must "hear" the feeling with which he spoke. The sermons of his last decade describe the God to whom human beings can relate as infinitely loving,

---

13. Syncrisis is a rhetorical figure in which two entities are simultaneously held together and separated. The verse Augustine quoted more frequently than any other, 1 Cor 13:12, engages this device: "We see now [*nunc*] through a dark glass; then [*tunc*] however, face to face."

14. *Conf*. 8.5.

Introduction

God-*is*-love, fundamentally incomprehensible, but in whom one can *participate* in a vast vortex of inclusive love. In short, the fervent and often repeated admonition in later years, whether he spoke to the educated Julian of Eclanum, or to illiterate members of his congregation, was: "If you can't understand, believe!" Belief, as Augustine understood the word, was not primarily intellectual assent, but the *feeling* of participating in God-is-love. It was this intimate response that he aimed to incite in preaching.[15] Possidius admired both the quantity and quality of Augustine's writings, but I think that he referred to Augustine's ability to communicate feeling when he observed:

> I think that those who gained most from him were those who had been able actually to see and hear him as he spoke in church.[16]

Second, *humility* was a favorite theme of Augustine's, recurring again and again in his sermons, treatises, and letters. Augustine considered humility the *sine qua non* of the Christian life. He remarked that if he had not discovered the importance of humility, "it was my soul that would have been lost."[17] Augustine did not urge his hearers to endeavor to *understand* God—don't even try! he said, in effect. God is beyond human reason, beyond even the ability of the strongest human imagination to grasp. Perhaps it is even more surprising that he also did not urge his congregation to seek the brief moments of spiritual vision he himself had

---

15. "Belief" is a word whose public meaning is presently abraded in Western societies. "I believe," rather than expressing a conviction so strong and integrated that I wager my values and my life on it, has acquired a weakened version in common usage. "I believe" presently signifies hesitancy, a confession of uncertainty; we use it when we wish to acknowledge doubt on a matter. We say of something of which we are confident, "I know." Yet contemporary usage requires the scientific method of testing hypotheses as a criterion of objective knowledge, thereby excluding religious knowledge, which is necessarily subjective, a matter of conviction, not of tested hypotheses. See chapter 1 n. 31 for Augustine's usage.

16. Possidius, *Uita* 31.9.

17. *Conf.* 7.20.

Introduction

experienced.[18] Rather, in the sermons of his last decade, he urged, "If you would see God, God is love."[19]

The ubiquity and stability of these themes *across* Augustine's writings reveal and emphasize Augustine's urgent attention to *this life*. He did not admonish his hearers to adopt attitudes and behavior presumed to assure a pleasurable posthumous life. In fact, the doctrines he defended in old age were precisely the doctrines that *insist* that there is nothing, literally *nothing*—neither good deeds nor tireless entreaty—that can affect one's eternal destiny. Moreover, Augustine's vivid awareness of the vulnerability and unpredictability of human intentions makes self-determination impossible.

> Perfect righteousness would come about *if* there were brought to bear the will sufficient for such an achievement; and that might be, *if* all the requirements of righteousness were known to us, and *if* they inspired in the soul such delight as to overcome the obstacle set by any other pleasure of pain. . . . For we are well aware that the extent of a person's knowledge is not in his own power, and that he will not follow what he knows to be worth pursuing unless he delight in it no less than it deserves his love . . . not to forget that we often go wrong in the belief that what we do is pleasing or not pleasing to God . . . and we see now darkly but then "face to face." . . . So, as it appears to me in the righteousness that is to be made perfect, much progress in this life has been made by one who knows how far he is from the perfection of righteousness.[20]

Not only do we human beings "see darkly," but we are also perennially at the mercy of rogue feelings that cannot be trusted to propel us in the direction of our best good: "Who can embrace wholeheartedly what gives him no delight? But who can determine for himself that what will delight him will come his way, and when it comes, that it should, in fact, delight him?"[21]

18. *Conf.* 9.10; 10.40.
19. *Ep. Io. tr.* 9.10.
20. *Spir. et litt.* 64; trans. Burnaby, *Spirit and the Letter*.
21. *Ad Simplicianum* 1.2.21; trans. Burleigh, *To Simplicianus*.

Introduction

"Leave it to God," Augustine urged again and again.[22] The doctrines of predestination and perseverance make that imperative stunningly clear. St. Augustine unqualifiedly bars the presumption and impossibility of attempting to take responsibility for oneself in this important determination. If a person's afterlife destiny could be influenced by effort, persuasion, or bribery, then self-pride—Augustine's nemesis of Christian life—would be the inevitable result. In fact, preoccupation with one's eternal destiny distracts from a Christian's *present* business. "Leave it to God," St. Augustine said, and place your attention on living lovingly in the body of Christ here and now.

Augustine's advocacy of humility is useful, not only to Augustine's congregation, but also to his twenty-first century readers. As interpreters of Augustine's writings, we inevitably bring our own experience, education, and cultural assumptions to understanding the old Augustine's words (usually in translation). One such cultural preconception is ageism, the "silent thought"[23] that old people are tired and tedious. We have *sometimes,* perhaps even often, observed this stereotype of old age "on location," so we surmise its universal applicability. However, if we are to learn from the perspectives of others, we must curb our culturally sponsored certitudes. Augustine did not, to my knowledge,[24] (bother to) argue that old age *can* afford extensive knowledge gained from rich experience. His sermons, and other writings of his last decade, simply *demonstrate* his understanding of the people *with whom* he spoke.[25] For example, he complained of his ailments but as a skilled rhetorician, he intentionally *used* his maladies to *connect*

---

22. *Perseu.* 11.25.

23. Michel Foucault's phrase for an unexamined assumption that "silently" influences thinking.

24. Cataloguing Augustine's library, Possidius commented that it was so voluminous that no one could read it all. Shortly after Augustine's death, Vincent of Lehrins remarked that if someone tells you he has read all of Augustine's writings, you know immediately that he is a liar!

25. Augustine's translators very frequently attribute faults they identify in the writings of Augustine's last decade to his old age, even dating sermons by "a certain grandfatherly tone"; see chapter 3 n. 29.

Introduction

with his hearers, to establish his consanguinity with his companions in the body of Christ.

The sermons of St. Augustine's old age are verdant with love and joy, and with compassion for the difficulty of believing.[26] He sought to explain, to clarify, and to find the metaphors and analogies that *help* belief, but above all, he sought to *share his feeling* of God's surrounding love with his companions in the body of Christ. These were sermons whose purpose was not to stimulate and cultivate intellectual assent, but to evoke and encourage the *feeling* of belief—that is, love of God and neighbor.

---

26. Carol Harrison's *The Art of Listening in the Early Church* is a learned and insightful discussion of the importance of listening in the largely illiterate societies of the early Christian era; Kevin Grove's *Augustine on Memory* also examines Augustine's sermons as spaces in which he came to understand and to describe the body of Christ as Christians' primary arena of self-identity.

Chapter One

The Inner Eye of the Beholder
St. Augustine on Miracles

Quanto magis ipse ineffabilis, qui talia demonstrauit.[1]
What can be shown cannot be said.[2]

AUGUSTINE'S VIEW OF THE value of miracles changed dramatically across an approximately thirty-year period of his life. In 391 CE he said that miracles were necessary in an early stage of Christianity in order to prompt belief "before anyone was fit to reason about divine and invisible things," but that miracles were no longer needed.[3] In the 420s, however, he enthusiastically supported the authentication and publication of contemporary miracles. His about-face on miracles, articulated primarily in his fifth-century sermons, was grounded on an integration of his theology, his pastoral experience, and his *feeling*.

---

1. *S.* 117.7; Hill, *Sermons* III/4, 214.
2. Wittgenstein, *Tractus Logico Philosophicus* 4.1212.
3. *Uera rel.* 25.47; trans. Burleigh, *St. Augustine*, 43.

Beautiful Bodies

A striking change in St. Augustine's view of miracles is evident in his writings across an approximately thirty-year period. He stated his early understanding of miracles in *De uera religione* (390 CE):

> We have heard that our predecessors, at a stage in faith on the way from temporal things up to eternal things, followed visible miracles, [however], *miracles were not allowed to continue to our time, lest the mind should always seek visible things*. . . . At that time the problem was to get people to believe before anyone was fit to reason about divine and invisible things.[4]

In Book XXII of *De ciuitatis dei*, written several years before his death, Augustine reconsidered his earlier position. He acknowledged that "miracles are being wrought even now in Christ's name," and he enthusiastically advocated and contributed to the recognition and publication of current miracles, declaring himself "extremely angry" when a healing miracle of which he had heard received no publicity.[5]

Reasons for St. Augustine's changed interest in miracles have been proposed. The British historian A. H. M. Jones suggested that his late enthusiasm about miracles represented a "collapse into popular credulity."[6] Others have proposed that he saw, in the fourth-century influx of "the whole world" into the Christian church, conditions similar to those of the formation of the earliest church when miracles effectively persuaded people to believe. This chapter will suggest a different interpretation, an interpretation that is possible due to Augustine's unique willingness to reveal his inner life—his thought and his feeling—to his congregation and, although he couldn't have predicted it, to his future readers.

St. Augustine's ideas, attitudes, and values were revised throughout his life both subtly and, in the case of miracles, dramatically. His about-face on the significance and value of miracles is an

---

4. *Uera rel.* 25.47; trans. Burleigh, *St. Augustine*, 43 (emphasis added).

5. *Ciu.* 22.8: "vehementer stomacharer"—an admission of anger I have not found elsewhere in Augustine's writings; trans. Dyson, *City of God*, 1125.

6. Jones, *Later Roman Empire*, 963–64.

example of his commitment to learning "by my own experience."[7] He consistently advocated humility, the disposition in which learning occurs; he considered its antithesis—pride—deadly, precisely because it prevents learning: "He who has convinced himself that he already knows, cannot learn."[8] Yet, there is fundamental continuity in St. Augustine's *theology* of miracles from his first treatise as a priest to his last writings.

Theological continuity strongly suggests that his *experience* must be considered the source of his changed conclusions regarding contemporary miracles. Augustine's change of heart on the value of miracles relied, not on ideas or beliefs that prompted a change of mind, but on his poignant *feeling* for human struggle and vulnerability. His own physical vulnerability, mentioned frequently in the sermons of his last decade, gave him an aperture through which to share others' weakness. Far from being a "collapse into popular credulity," his revised appreciation of miracles revealed deepened consanguinity with the people to whom he preached.

For St. Augustine, thinking and feeling were not separable activities. Augustine lived many centuries before Descartes declared a separation between thought and feeling, mind and body.[9] As if Augustine cannily foresaw that he must emphasize the unity of thinking and feeling for much later readers who might assume their separability, his description of *feeling* as an essential component of thinking makes this clear. Reading the Roman philosopher and rhetorician Cicero, when he was nineteen years old, "I was urged on and inflamed with a passionate zeal to love and seek and obtain and embrace and hold fast wisdom herself." An inner fire suddenly and irrevocably "altered my way of feeling" (*mutauit affectum meum*), he wrote.[10]

---

7. *Conf.* 4.2; also 7.16; 8.5; trans. Warner, *Confessions*, 56, 153, 168.

8. *Util. cred.* 11.25; trans. Meagher, *Advantage of Believing*, 425.

9. Sheets Johnstone, arguing for the irreducible unity of person, writes of mind and body: "there is no 'they'" (*Corporeal Turn*, 20).

10. *Conf.* 3.4; Warner translation, slightly altered, *Confessions*, 56; wisdom (*sapientia*) is gendered feminine in Latin; Hockenbery, "He, She, and It," 435.

Similarly, revised ideas did not prompt his cataclysmic conversion to celibacy; he repeated several times in the preamble to his account: "my mind was made up." Rather, he emphasized his feeling, expressed in his body: "my forehead, cheeks, eyes, the color of my face and inflection of voice expressed my mind better than the words I used. . . . I wept . . . my bones cried out. . . . I tore my hair, beat my forehead, locked my fingers together, clasped my knee."[11] As his tension resolved, he observed: "My face changed. . . . [It] was now perfectly calm [*tranquillo iam uultu*]."[12] He *felt* the small muscles in his face relax. St. Augustine could not be more emphatically insistent that his experience of conversion engaged the whole person.

Feeling—physical, intellectual, and emotional—gathered and expressed St. Augustine's subjectivity. Throughout his life, weeping demonstrated the intensity of his feeling.[13] From the frustrated tears of the infant, unable to communicate his desires to his caregivers,[14] to the young adult, struggling to *choose* among desires he considered incompatible,[15] to the dying man, weeping in meditation copiously and constantly (*ubertime et iugitur*),[16] the strongest experiences of Augustine's life were marked by tears.

Countless examples in Augustine's writings testify to his conviction that feeling is an essential component of thinking.[17] The most frequent and vivid examples occur in Augustine's fifth-century sermons. As discussed below, Augustine's preaching, especially his sermons on the psalms (*en. ps.*), his homilies on the Gospel of John (*Io. eu. tr.*), and the First Epistle of John (*ep. Io. tr.*), are laced with examples. Feeling also played a central role in his later esteem of contemporary miracles.

11. *Conf.* 8.12; trans. Warner, *Confessions*, 182.

12. *Conf.* 8.12; trans. Warner, *Confessions*, 183.

13. Miles, *Reading Augusting on Memory*, chapter 1, "Augustine: Theologian of Feeling," 1–18.

14. *Conf.* 1.6.

15. *Conf.* 8.8; 8.12.

16. Possidius, *Uita* 31; trans. Weiskotten, 56–57.

17. Damasio, *Feeling and Knowing*, 7.

The Inner Eye of the Beholder

AUGUSTINE'S EARLY THEOLOGY OF MIRACLES

> I call a miracle anything that appears difficult or unusual, *beyond the expectations or comprehension of the one who marvels at it.*[18]

The first treatise Augustine wrote after his ordination to the priesthood, *The Advantage of Believing* (*util. cred.*, 391 CE), placed his discussion of miracles within his earliest description of his own conversion to Catholic faith, predating his more detailed account in *Confessions* by approximately a decade.[19] Although he later elaborated the theology of miracles described in *util. cred.*, it remained essentially unchanged throughout his writings.[20] In brief, miracles exhibit God's power.

Augustine wrote *util. cred.* in part to denounce the Manichaean teachings to which he had been attracted before his conversion to Catholic Christianity. He was seduced, he said, by Manichaean claims to provide *reason* for their doctrines rather than to require belief. In retrospect, he commented ruefully, "Who would not be enticed by these promises?," citing the attraction reason held for "a youthful mind, desirous of truth . . . haughty and talkative . . . myself."[21]

However, as a Manichaean hearer, Augustine found himself exhausted and dehydrated (*exhaustus et aridus*).[22] He learned "by my own experience"[23] that reason alone does not nourish the whole person; he returned to the church for nourishment, "weeping

---

18. *Util. cred.* 16.34; trans. Meagher, *Advantage of Believing*, 438.

19. *Util. cred.* 8.20–21; trans. Meagher, *Advantage of Believing*, 415–16. Augustine's earliest description of his conversion to celibacy—the *util. cred.* account—did not include the vivid physical and emotional struggle of his later account in *conf.* 8.8–12.

20. Significantly, in his maturity Augustine did not repeat the theological rationale for the disappearance of miracles that he offered in *util. cred.*, namely that miracles ceased "lest the mind should always seek visible things."

21. *Util. cred.* 1.2; trans. Meagher, *Advantage of Believing*, 392.

22. *Util. cred.* 393.

23. *Conf.* 4 2; 8.5; 7.16; trans. Warner, *Confessions*, 70, 153, 168.

Beautiful Bodies

and groaning deeply." His image is violent; desperately he "beat the breasts [of the church] . . . wrung them out that there might trickle forth just enough nourishment to refresh me."[24] Having learned that impeccable reasoning does not guarantee truth, he advised the friend to whom he dedicated the treatise that, rather than pursuing reason, he should identify "the certain few (people) whose beliefs and lifestyle exhibit truth." You know what truth is, he wrote, "if you know among whom it is."[25]

In short, reason had lost the indubitable authority of Augustine's pre-baptism dialogues. Yet belief in miracles must not be credulous. Reasonable belief began with Jesus's miracles:[26] "Since it is not easy to recognize [Jesus] through reason . . . it was necessary to present certain miracles to the eyes . . . so that moved by authority, people's lives and habits might first be purged, and thus become amenable to the acceptance of reason."[27] Jesus's miracles altered the credible grounds for belief *from reason to authority*. "What wasn't seen, wasn't as a rule believed"; by these temporal benefits that were seen, "he was building up faith in the things that were not seen."[28] The church, he wrote, inherited the "highest authority" (*culmen auctoritatis*) established by Jesus's miracles: "through his miracles he gained authority, through his authority he won faith, through faith he drew the multitude."[29] Augustine described his own "reasonable" belief: "I believed the widespread report of peoples and nations . . . a report which had the strength of numbers, agreement, and antiquity."[30]

Reason, he conceded, is valuable in its arena of accountability, that is, verifiable knowledge; but even then, reason is dependent on language, and words are too frangible to entrust with the inherently untestable, unprovable, and yet supremely important sphere

---

24. *Conf.* 8.12; trans. Warner, *Confessions*, 182.
25. *Util. cred.* 7.16; Meagher, *Advantage of Believing*, 410.
26. *Util. cred.* 14.32; Meagher, *Advantage of Believing*, 434.
27. *Util. cred.* 15.33; Meagher, *Advantage of Believing*, 435.
28. *S.* 88.1; trans. Hill, *Sermons* III/3, 419.
29. *S.* 17.35; Meagher, *Advantage of Believing*, 440.
30. *Util. cred.* 14.32; Meagher, *Advantage of Believing*, 434.

The Inner Eye of the Beholder

of religion: thus, "what we understand we owe to reason, what we believe, to authority." "We believe," he wrote, "and we believe without any doubt, *what we admit we cannot know.*"[31] "Reasonable belief" must be based on trustworthy authority; belief must be credible, not credulous.[32]

Clearly, St. Augustine did not jettison reason; rather, he had become convinced that belief is not primarily a matter of intellectual assent. Even the rare person who may be "fit to reason" must first believe:

> Unless he first believes . . . and shows the mind of a suppliant, obeying certain important and necessary precepts, and completely purging himself by a certain way of life, he will not in any other way attain to that which is pure truth.[33]

Moreover, St. Augustine recognized that core Christian beliefs are neither "reasonable" nor experiential. Jesus's miracle of raising Lazarus from the dead (John 11:19, 33, 35) provides scriptural authority for belief in the resurrection of the bodies, but neither personal experience nor contemporary eyewitness testimony can be marshalled to support belief in Jesus's incarnation and resurrection, much less in the resurrection of all humans to reward or punishment.[34] Miracles are needed to prompt belief in this mind-boggling creedal assertion: "many miracles were wrought in order to testify to that one grand and saving miracle of Christ's ascension into heaven in the flesh in which he rose. . . . (Miracles) bear

---

31. *Util. cred.* 12.26; trans. Meagher, *Advantage of Believing*, 427 (emphasis added). Augustine distinguished between ordinary language and more precise philosophical and theological language: "When we use words better suited to common usage, as *the holy Scripture uses them*, we should not hesitate to say that we know both what we perceive with the bodily senses and what we believe on the authority of trustworthy witnesses" (*retr.* 1.14.3). See also Catherine Conybeare, *Irrational Augustine*, and Robert P. Kennedy's review in *Augustinian Studies*.

32. *Util. cred.* 16.34; trans. Meagher, *Advantage of Believing*, 438.

33. *Util. cred.* 10.24; trans. Meagher, *Advantage of Believing*, 421.

34. *Ciu.* 22.21; trans. Dyson, *City of God*, 1152.

witness to the faith that preaches the resurrection of the flesh to life."[35]

St. Augustine understood the difficulty of believing a doctrine so distant from experience.[36] Yet, far from minimizing, marginalizing, or explaining away resurrection of the body, his *Ep.* 263 to the consecrated virgin, Sapida (written to comfort her on the death of her brother), emphasized its literal concreteness. When a loved one dies, Augustine wrote, "the heart is pierced and tears come forth like heart's blood," but because of the hope of bodily resurrection, unique to Christians, "the sorrow of believers for their dear dead should not be of long duration."[37]

In 391 CE, however, Augustine still harbored hope that eventually "the many" would come to believe in God's power (*uirtutem Dei*) without contemporary miracles: "not only many learned men . . . but also a multitude of unlearned men and women . . . both believe and assert . . . that [God] can be reached only by the intellect."[38] He anticipated that reason would eventually replace miracles. Further pastoral experience did not substantiate this hope.

Augustine's Sermons

St. Augustine's fifth-century sermons demonstrate two—not new, but noticeably strengthened—interrelated and interdependent motifs. First, he acknowledged both the necessity and the difficulty of belief for many people and thus, the importance of miracles to prompt and consolidate belief. Second, he repeatedly emphasized his own *primary* self-identification, not as the aggregate of the events and choices of his personal life, but as his solidarity with his congregation as a member of the body of Christ.

35. *Ciu.* 21.7–8; trans. Dyson, *City of God*, 1061.

36. Augustine's learned and respected antagonist, the Platonist Porphyry, found the resurrection of body the most objectionable Christian belief; discussed in chapter 5; see also Thomas Clemens, "Augustine and Porphyry."

37. *Ep.* 263; discussed further in chapter 5. See also Grote and Müller, "Augustinus," 113–41.

38. *Util. cred.* 17.35; trans. Meagher, *Advantage of Believing*, 439.

The Inner Eye of the Beholder

First, Augustine's urgent interest in assisting belief is evident in the most often repeated phrases of his late sermons: "Do not try to understand in order to believe, but believe in order to understand" (quoting Isaiah 7:9). "Let the one who can, understand; let the one who cannot understand, believe."[39] Belief became, for Augustine, not only a viable alternative to understanding, but its necessary precondition. His last correspondence, unfinished at his death, strongly advised Julian of Eclanum—one who certainly could be considered "fit to reason"—"if you cannot understand this, believe it!"[40]

Second, St. Augustine became demonstrably more empathetic with the people to whom he preached. The attentive reader of Augustine's early sermons detects a tone of patient instruction; he *taught* his hearers. However, those of his later years have a personal, conversational quality not evident in earlier sermons. Whether he preached in the large Basilica Pacis at Hippo, the Carthage cathedral, or in more casual settings, such as Sunday afternoon homilies in the churchyard, Augustine's sermons had a more intimate tone.[41] Shunning an authoritative posture, he positioned himself as one of the people, often pausing to respond to their reactions: "Why this cheering, why this excitement, why this show of love?"[42] "Why did you all shout and applaud, if not because you got the point?"[43] Less frequently, he asked, "Would your graces please pay just a little attention, and not make such a racket with each other?"[44]

Augustine's late sermons referred again and again to his own limitations—physical, intellectual, and spiritual.[45] This rhetorical

---

39. *Io. eu. tr.* 29.6, also 36.7; trans. Hill, *Gospel of John 1–40*; trans. Hill, *Sermons* III/12, 493.

40. *C. Iul. opus imperf.* 4.104.

41. Harrison, *Art of Listening*, 122.

42. *Io. eu. tr.* 3.21; trans. Hill, *Gospel of John 1–40*; trans. Hill, *Sermons* III/12, 84.

43. *Io. eu. tr.* 18.8, 328.

44. *S.* 126.8; trans. Hill, *Sermons* III/4, 274.

45. Augustine explained in one of his last sermons: "As you see, I am now old in years, but as far as ill health goes, I have been old for a long time"; *S.* 355.7; trans. Hill, *Sermons* III/10, 170.

Beautiful Bodies

tool, used by classical rhetoricians to establish a speaker's rapport with his audience, was more than rhetoric for Augustine. It was a profound theological verity. No longer the young man who wrote his *Confessions*, eagerly rehearsing his personal experience in order to detect God's inner leading, he now identified him*self* as "communally constructed," a member of the Body of Christ.[46] He invited his congregation to think *with* him, to evaluate the truth of his interpretation, or to understand the Scripture of the day differently.[47] He was intensely aware that a sermon's effectiveness depends not only on the preacher's skill, but also on the hearers' ability to *hear* his words with their inner ears: "Do you not have ears in the heart . . . do you not have eyes in the heart? Your heart both sees and hears."[48] His sermons address his congregants' inner ears.

> Given my limitations I grasp what I set before you; when the door is opened, I am nourished together with you; when it is shut, I knock together with you.[49]

> I have set you a problem that bothers me. Yes, it bothers me a lot.[50]

> And so, my dearest friends, let me tell you what I think about the subject, without prejudging anything better that you may have perceived . . . this is my opinion and it is for you to see whether what I think is true, or comes close to the truth.[51]

> All this has not been said by little me.[52]

---

46. Grove, *Augustine on Memory*, Part I, chapter 2, "Preaching from the Whole," 57–82. Discussed further in Centerpiece.

47. The empathy of Augustine's later preaching may also relate to his strengthened doctrine of original sin, a profound and sympathetic acknowledgment that all human beings suffer and struggle under a debilitating burden.

48. *Io. eu. tr.* 18.10; trans. Hill, *Gospel of John 1–40*, 330.

49. *Io. eu. tr.* 39.

50. *Io. eu. tr.* 4.16, 99.

51. *Io. eu. tr.* 16.3, 298.

52. *Io. eu. tr.* 1.17, 53.

Stretch your minds, please, help my poverty of language.[53]

Pay close attention to what I want to say, even if I cannot do it very well.[54]

You work at standing and listening; I work even harder to stand and speak. . . . I am too tired to go on talking."[55]

CONTEMPORARY MIRACLES

St. Augustine's fifth-century sermons acknowledge several kinds of miracles: 1) ordinary miracles, seen everyday; 2) extraordinary miracles, including miracles that are either evident to the senses, or silent and invisible, such as healing miracles; and 3) inner miracles.[56]

Everyday Miracles

Augustine was more eager to encourage his hearers to notice ordinary miracles than he was to marvel at extraordinary miracles.[57] Sermon 130 (after 426 CE), on the miracle of the loaves and fishes (John 6:5–14), reminded his hearers that ordinary miracles are a direct extension of Jesus's miracles, evidence of God's power: "The one who multiplied the five loaves is the one who multiplies the

---

53. *S.* 119.34; trans. Hill, *Sermons* III/4, 228.
54. *Io. eu. tr.* 20.3; trans. Hill, *Gospel of John, 1–40*, 359.
55. *Io. eu. tr.* 1.19.17, 53.
56. See Jean-Michel Roessli, "Mirabilia, miraculum," for an alternative categorization of miracles (physical, psychological, and theological) considered by St. Augustine.
57. Plotinus also commented on habituation to everyday miracles: "We encounter the extraordinary with astonishment, though we should be astonished at these ordinary things too if we were unfamiliar with them" (*Ennead* 4.4.37; trans. Armstrong, *Plotinus*, 255). Wittgenstein noted: "One is unable to notice something because it is always before one's eye. . . . And this means we fail to be struck by what . . . is most striking and powerful" (*Philosophical Investigations*, no. 129).

Beautiful Bodies

seeds germinating in the ground, so that comparatively few seeds are sown and great granaries are filled. Because this occurs every year, nobody is astonished."[58]

Miracles are not only familiar, they are *too* familiar, so that they are not noticed. They are easily *perceived*, but we fail to *see* them as evidence of God's power. Augustine said that extraordinary miracles would not be needed if we noticed the marvels of everyday life.

> Consider the changes of day and night, the very constant order of heavenly bodies, the fourfold change of the seasons, the fall of leaves and their return to the trees the following Spring, the infinite power in seeds, the beauty of light, and the variety of colors, sounds, smells, and tastes. . . . But we have little respect for all these things . . . surely because we constantly experience them.[59]

> God has made a world full of innumerable marvels, in sky, earth, air, and waters, while the earth itself is beyond doubt a miracle greater and more excellent than all the wonders with which it is filled.[60]

> You know how to marvel at unusual things; are they greater than the things you're accustomed to see? People were amazed at the Lord Jesus Christ giving so many thousands their fill on five loaves, and they are not amazed at the land being filled with crops from a few grains. What was water became wine; people saw; they were dumbfounded. What else is done with the rain through the roots of the vine?[61]

> God's miracles have grown cheap in our estimation through their regularity, so that almost no one bothers to pay attention to the wonderful and stupendous action of God in every grain of seed.[62]

58. *S.* 130.3; trans. Hill, *Sermons* III. 4, 312.
59. *Util. cred.* 16.34; trans. Meagher, *Advantage of Believing*, 437.
60. *Ciu.* 22.8; trans. Dyson, *City of God*, 1120.
61. *S.* 126.4; trans. Hill, *Sermons* III/4, 271.
62. *S.* 24.1.

The Inner Eye of the Beholder

Augustine's most striking example of ordinary miracles is human birth, which launches the miracle of human beings: "God's daily miracle . . . [is] that a human being, who was not, should . . .by being born, appear in light of day. Could anything be as wonderful as that, as difficult to comprehend? Marvel at such things, sit up and take notice."[63]

Augustine startlingly remarked in several late sermons that human birth is an even greater miracle than Jesus's resurrection:

> One man rises from the dead; all marvel; many are born daily, and no one marvels! If we thought about it a little more rationally, it is a more wonderful miracle for someone who did not exist just to be, than for someone who already existed to come back to life.[64]

> Making a human being, after all, is certainly a greater miracle than resuscitating one. But because nobody was moved to wonder at his making them every day, he showed himself occasionally resuscitating them.[65]

God's all-time best miracle is human beings:

> People see extraordinary things and are amazed. Where do the people themselves come from, to be amazed? Where were they? Where have they come from? Where does the body get its shape and the variety of its limbs and organs?[66]

> You, the marveler, yourself are an amazing miracle. . . . He came to do extraordinary things in order to help you recognize the hand of your maker in these ordinary things as well. . . . He came to raise the dead, to everyone's amazement to restore to the light a person who was in

---

63. S. 130.4; trans. Hill, *Sermons* III/4, 313; the translator gives the Latin *pauca grana* (little seeds) an interpretation that Augustine certainly did not intend: "[God] has made horrid, slimy seeds into human beings."

64. *Io. eu. tr.* 8.1; 9.1; trans. Hill, *Gospel of John 1–40*, 168; also S. 242.

65. S. 374.11; trans. Hill, *Sermons* III/10, 376.

66. S. 242.1; also *Io. eu. tr.* 32.3; trans. Hill, *Gospel of John 1–40*.

the light, while every day he brings into the light of day those who didn't exist at all.[67]

Men go abroad to marvel at the heights of mountains, the huge waves of the sea, the broad streams of rivers, the vastness of the ocean, the turnings of the stars—and they do not notice themselves.[68]

Extraordinary Miracles

Extraordinary miracles, the miracles that "everyone sees," Augustine said, are only as valuable as their inner effects. Preaching on the parable of the guest who lacked a wedding garment, Augustine said that the "wedding garment" that grants admission to the feast is not miracles: "So what is the wedding garment? . . . [It is] love from a pure heart, a good conscience, and an unfeigned faith (1 Tim 1:5). That is the wedding garment."[69]

In fact, Augustine repeated, unusual miracles are not greater than daily miracles:

> [Miracles] amaze people who have ceased to value those that occur every day . . . even those things which are known to us most commonly in the natural order are no less wonderful, and would be a source of astonishment to all who consider them, if men were not accustomed to be amazed at nothing except what is rare.[70]

Traces of Augustine's youthful skepticism are evident in his mature caution regarding miracles. He insisted that he did not "rashly" (*temere*) believe all the miracles reported to him; he believed only "those I have experienced myself *and which anyone can*

---

67. *S.* 126.4; trans. Hill, *Sermons* III/4, 271.

68. *Conf.* 10.8; trans. Warner, *Confessions*, 217.

69. *S.* 90.5–6; trans. Hill, *Sermons* III/3, 451. Augustine's interest in miracles intruded in this sermon in which miracles had little to do with the pericope of the day, Matt 22:1–14.

70. *Io. eu. tr.* 24.1; trans. Hill, *Gospel of John 1–40*, 423.

easily experience."[71] He could "neither deny nor affirm" many of the accounts of miracles he received.[72] Moreover, he was careful to say that God is not the author of all miracles; miracles can also be produced by demons, or by "men using the demonic arts."[73] Indeed, some miracles that seem to be contrary to nature, he said, are simply "contrary to nature *as we know it*."[74] In a society in which there was avid popular interest in miracles—often bordering on superstition—he may have seemed to many people more skeptical than credulous.

Inner Miracles

St. Augustine's most highly valued miracle was the miracle *no one sees,* the miracle of subjective (*intus*) change that Augustine himself had experienced. Some people, he said, "are amazed at visible miracles and have no idea that there is a greater kind. Others hear about the miracles performed on bodies and now have a greater admiration for those performed on souls."[75] For "*the inner miracle is greater than the outer* one that everyone sees."[76] Inner miracles *change the person in whom they occur.* Not only is the interior miracle invisible, it also defies description:

> God does something in us, I do not know what, in a spiritual, non-material way; it is neither a sound to strike the ears, nor a color to be distinguished by the eyes, nor a smell to be picked up by the nostrils, nor a flavor to be judged by the palate, nor something hard or soft to be perceived by touching it; it is easy to *feel* (*sentire facile est*) and impossible to explain (*explicare impossibile est*).[77]

---

71. *Ciu.* 21.7; Dyson, *City of God,* 1120 (emphasis added).
72. *Ciu.* 21.8; Dyson, *City of God,* 1066.
73. *Ciu.* 21.6; Dyson, *City of God,* 1056.
74. *Ciu.* 21.8; Dyson, *City of God,* 1061 (emphasis added).
75. *S.* 98.1; trans. Hill, *Sermons* III/4, 43.
76. *Io. eu. tr.* 40.3, italics added; trans. Hill, *Gospel of John 1–40,* 595.
77. *Io. eu. tr.* 40.5, 598–99.

Beautiful Bodies

An inner miracle is "impossible to explain," but *you know it when you feel it*—it is "easy to feel." Furthermore, a certain spiritual affinity is necessary for recognizing an interior miracle in someone else: "Not all have the ability to see those who are dead in the heart rise again; to see that you need to have already risen in the heart yourself."[78]

Ultimately, however ardently Augustine struggled to express his understanding of God's activity *intus*, he was forced to confess not only his own inability, but the ultimate inability of language itself to describe this mystery: "if you can grasp it, it isn't God"; "God is unutterable"; "these matters remain inexpressible."[79] The appropriate human response to God's inscrutability, Augustine said, is humility.

As a much younger man, Augustine had learned humility from Jesus, whose humility, he wrote in his *Confessions*, was fully demonstrated by his willingness to accept a human body.[80] Much later, he quoted Matt 11:29, "Learn from me, because I am gentle and humble of heart," commenting, "that is the sum total of the medicine required to heal us. . . . What good does it do you if you can perform miracles, and are proud, and not gentle and humble of heart?"[81] Humility remained the linchpin of St. Augustine's later sermons.

In old age Augustine understood that bodies *incarnate* humility. Every life begins and closes in helplessness, fragility, and vulnerability. Aged bodies, redolent of a common humanity, marginalize individual achievement, reinforcing awareness of human solidarity. In old age Augustine espoused a complex humility, both personally unpretentious and gloriously aggregated as "becoming Christ."

---

78. *S.* 98.1; trans. Hill, *Sermons* III/4, 43.

79. *S.* 117.5; 7; 12; trans. Hill, *Sermons* III/4; 211, 213, 216.

80. *Conf.* 7.17; trans. Warner, *Confessions*, 154. Even humility requires discernment. Augustine warned against humility that "thinks too little of himself," causing crippling despair; *util. cred.* 10.24; trans. Meagher, *Advantage of Believing*, 421.

81. *Io. eu. tr.* 142.11; trans. Hill, *Gospel of John*.

CONCLUSION

Augustine's reversal regarding the usefulness of miracles must not be emphasized to the extent of ignoring the continuity of his *theology* of miracles; the demonstration of God's power was the continuing basis of Augustine's understanding of miracles. The world's belief—a miracle in itself—was not the result of human persuasion, he wrote, but of divine power: "God can do what to the unbeliever is impossible."[82] Augustine learned from "my own experience" the value of miracles, *especially* those seen everyday, and the inner miracle that alters feeling, that most intimate characteristic (*mutauit affectum meum*).

St. Augustine's candid and vivid descriptions of his thoughts, actions, and feelings enable his readers to imagine the inner life of a fourth-century Christian bishop, passionately and thoughtfully lived. Propelled—pushed—by relentless restlessness in his youth, he was increasingly attracted, drawn, *pulled* by the God he called beauty, life, and love. In the wealth of his writing and preaching, readers experience the emotional urgency of his life, from the infant at his mother's breast, to the dying man weeping alone in meditation, reliving *in feeling* the miracle that was God doing something in his life that was "easy to feel and impossible to explain."

---

82. *Ciu.* 21.5–6; trans. Dyson, *City of God*, 1057.

Chapter Two

St. Augustine's Last Desire

IN HIS LAST YEARS, Augustine's correspondence reveals his impatience with doctrinal questions and requests for advice on practical matters of ecclesiastical discipline. Scholars have often attributed his uncharacteristic reluctance to address these matters to the diminishing competence and energy of old age. This chapter demonstrates that his evident unwillingness to respond to such queries relates rather to his desire to sequester increased time for meditation. Throughout his Christian life he described and refined his practice of meditation; it gathered urgent importance as he neared death. In meditation he sought to recall in detail God's loving leading *within* the chaos and pain of his youthful desires and throughout his life. I explore his understanding of "God is love" from his earliest (extant) treatise, *De beata vita* (*beata u.*; 386 CE), his Easter sermons on First John (415 CE), to his *Enchiridion* (*ench.*; 421 CE) as the core of his developing understanding of God's activity in himself (Augustine), a member of the body of Christ.

In his middle years, St. Augustine gave unstintingly of his time and energy to doctrinal controversy and to requests for his advice on various matters relating to Christian belief and practice. However, letters, treatises, and sermons of his last decade reveal that he was tired of argument, that he wanted to be quit of quarrels and repetitious requests for explanation and advice. Augustine's characteristic eagerness to respond to "the care of endangered souls,"[1] had shifted, and a petulant tone emerged in his correspondence. For example, to the African tribune Dulcitius's request that Augustine rebut a Donatist tract he replied, "I am now extremely busy; [and] I have refuted this kind of nonsense in many other works of mine."[2] I suggest that St. Augustine's impatience can be understood, not as a result of diminished mental capacities due to old age, but rather as prompted by his felt urgency to set aside increased time for meditation. Awareness that death was approaching focused and strengthened his passion to know "God and the soul," first articulated when he was a catechumen.[3]

St. Augustine's efforts to decline writing assignments are remarkably similar to contemporary scholars' litany of excuses for demurring to write on an assigned or requested topic: he claimed insufficient knowledge; he repeatedly insisted that he preferred the interpretations of "more learned men" than himself; and he recommended others' writings on the proposed topic.[4] These tactics failed to deter the deacon Quodvultdeus's repeated request that he compose a compendium refuting Donatist beliefs. Recognizing that Augustine was "an old man who is thinking of higher things, administering more important things, and suffering bodily ailments," Quodvultdeus nevertheless dismissed Augustine's recommendation of verbose Greek authors.[5] Finally, lacking further excuses, Augustine simply refused, saying that he was too busy.

On other occasions Augustine cited ecclesiastical authority; "there is nothing like canonical authority; the creed should be

1. Brown, *Augustine*, 466.
2. *Ep.* 204.4.
3. *Sol.* 1.2.7; trans. Gilligan, *Soliloquies*, 350.
4. *Ep.* 222.2.
5. *Ep.* 221.4.

enough," he snapped.[6] He expounded the creed as a statement of his own beliefs in letters and sermons, and he wrote *Enchiridion* (421 CE), hoping that this exposition of Christian faith, hope, and love—"all you need to know"—would preclude further questions. "Just believe" he wrote to the exiled Pelagian bishop, Julian of Eclanum, "if you cannot understand this, believe it!"[7] This was a formula he repeated many times in his late correspondence. "Don't try to understand in order to believe, believe that you may understand."[8] Questions about incomprehensible matters, he said, "must be left to God."[9]

Ecclesiastical responsibilities also demanded Augustine's time and considered judgment. He was called upon to give advice on multiple matters, such as an internal schism in a convent.[10] His letter to Pope Celestine acknowledged that, "thinking of retiring," he had acted hastily and with a poor outcome in one of his duties as a bishop; he had recommended the ordination of a bishop who had not advanced through the clerical ranks as was usual.[11] His patience was sorely taxed when he was asked a question he considered unimportant. One hapless questioner asked about the nature and location of "the Lord's body in heaven"; Augustine declined to answer, saying that the question was "overcurious and superfluous."[12] The letters of his last decade reveal the questions, issues, and annoyances with which he was importuned; his sermons of the same period disclose his preoccupations as he neared death. In his late sermons, preached at the Basilica Pacis in Hippo, Augustine spoke intimately, humbly, as if with friends, to his congregation. He asked for their concentration and patience. Citing "an old man's feeble powers," he begged weariness: "I am too tired

---

6. *Dulc. qu.* 3.3, 3.3; trans. Defarrari, *Eight Questions*, 446, 448.
7. *c. Iul.* 4.104.
8. *Io. eu. tr.* 29.6: 33.5; 36.7.
9. *Perseu.* 11.25.
10. *Ep.* 211.
11. *Ep.* 209.10.
12. *F. et sym.* 6.13.

to go on talking," commenting, "an old man's sermon should be not only weighty but brief."[13] He repeatedly asked for their prayers.

Moreover, in 426 CE, four years before he died, St. Augustine asked that the priest Eraclius be appointed his successor so that he (Augustine) could be relieved of some of the duties by which, "both morning and afternoon I am enmeshed in men's affairs." He reminded his congregation that, by an "acclaimed, voted, and recorded" contractual understanding (Acts of the Councils of Numidia and Carthage, 416 CE), he had been formally granted a period of uninterrupted time for study. He reported that this agreement was honored for a short time, then summarily revoked. He asked that the "leisure" he had been promised be reinstated, assuring the congregation that his time will not be spent in idleness, but in intensive labor.[14] Still fearing interruptions, ten days before he died, he asked that no one except caregivers approach his bedside. His friend and biographer, Possidius, reported that his last request was granted, "so that he had all that time free for prayer."[15]

A further factor played a role in the old Augustine's reluctance to spend his diminishing time on the myriad issues vying for his attention. Augustine was both a bishop and a monk, and the responsibilities of each role were distinct. Bishops' days were largely spent in administrative duties, including, in Augustine's time, acting as judge in an episcopal court in which many kinds of disputes were adjudicated. As a monk he expected to spend long hours in prayer, fasting, and service to the monastic community.[16] His late publications, as well as his urgent request for the appointment of a successor who could begin to assume some of his duties provide strong evidence that nearing the end of his life, his self-identification as a monk gathered urgency.

The duties of bishops and monks were not incompatible; in fact, in the late fourth and fifth centuries, bishops were increasingly

13. *S.* 348.4; trans. Hill *Sermons* III/10, 94.
14. *Ep.* 213.5–6.
15. Possidius, *Uita*, 31; trans. Weiskotten, 56–57.
16. *Ep.* 211 is "regarded as the source of the Augustinian Rule"; Parsons, *Letters* V, 38.

Beautiful Bodies

chosen from monastic communities. Nevertheless, time management was challenging to one who was both. In Augustine's time, Christian leadership—both institutional and spiritual—was in process of pivoting from late antiquity in which (for approximately five hundred years), bishops and priests were Christianity's primary spokesmen, to the Western European medieval world in which (for five hundred or so years), monks were its primary exponents and interpreters.[17]

In Augustine's time, few monks were concerned with nuances of doctrine which, in fourth-century ecumenical councils, had primarily drawn the attention of clergy. Yet Augustine's ongoing engagement with revising and refining his practice of meditation indicates that throughout his ecclesiastical career he continued to think of himself—*intus*, "*essentially*"—as the monk he had never ceased to be since the moment of his conversion to celibacy. On returning to his birthplace in North Africa, Augustine founded several monasteries and lived in monastic community for the rest of his life.[18] During his busy years as a bishop, he "had" no time for meditation, but he *made* time for meditation, the first responsibility of a monk. If he had placed meditation at the bottom of his list of responsibilities, to be exercised when his duties as a bishop had been accomplished, he could seldom have meditated; however, his writings suggest that meditation was a priority, subordinating but never supplanting the responsibilities of a bishop. Yet, it was difficult to be both.[19]

17. See Claudia Rapp, *Holy Bishops in Late Antiquity*, on Augustine's role in a rapidly emerging ecclesiastical culture in which bishops sponsored clerical monasteries; see also Van Fleteren et al., "Editorial Conclusions," in which the editors describe "Augustine's enormous authority during the Christian Middle Ages. . . . To be Christian was to be Augustinian. Augustine was not in the mainstream; he defined the mainstream."

18. For monasteries founded by Augustine, see Lawless, *Augustine of Hippo*.

19. More than a century after Augustine, Gregory I (d. CE 604), pressed into service as the bishop of Rome after living for some time as a monk, struggled with disparate loyalties and duties. He regretted the loss of "all the beauty of that spiritual repose," lamenting that "the contact with worldly men and their affairs which is a necessary part of my duties as a bishop, has left my soul defiled with earthly activities"; see trans. Zimmerman, *Dialogues* I., 4.

St. Augustine's Last Desire

This chapter seeks to demonstrate that Augustine's old age cannot be understood without taking into consideration his long practice of meditation.[20] A great deal of contemporary thought and ink has been devoted to defining "meditation," "contemplation," and other spiritual exercises; that well-trodden ground cannot be revisited in this chapter, but I must indicate how I use the word. I do not define or characterize meditation as a general practice, but rather I reconstruct Augustine's particular practice, as he designed, refined, and practiced it throughout his Christian life.

Augustine's meditation consisted of several exercises. First, he described his study of Scripture as meditation (*studium, commentatio*); he did not merely understand scriptural words and phrases in their ordinary usage; he also probed their multiple significances, historical, prophetic and—most importantly—spiritual. Second, Augustine's meditation encompassed detailed gathering (*colligere*) of his memories in order to identify God's infallible leading *within* the chaos and apparent randomness of his life. As vividly described in his *Confessions,* he recognized God's intimate activity from earliest infancy and throughout his life. Third, meditation, as Augustine practiced it, included concentrated attentiveness (*cogitatio, intentio*) to *receiving* the meaning for which he prayed (*precatio*). Each was an essential feature of meditation for Augustine; together, these exercises were capable of producing an interior excitement Augustine repeatedly characterized as "fire." Common to these distinguishable exercises is a subjective inner relishing or savoring of both the process and the object of meditation that Augustine recognized by the *feeling* it generated: "I cannot even comprehend myself whom you have made; and yet in my meditation a fire flames out, so that I always seek your face."[21]

Augustine's meditation required both time and quiet. He acknowledged in a late sermon, "It is difficult to see Christ in a crowd; our minds need some solitude; someone who is attentive

---

20. Chapter 4, "St. Augustine's Tears," examines both his commitment to meditation and its refinement across his Christian life. This chapter anticipates that more detailed discussion.

21. *Trin.* 15.7.13; trans. McKenna, *St. Augustine,* 181.

Beautiful Bodies

in solitude may see God."[22] He sought to see God through meditation, and meditation permeated and informed his theology, his preaching, and his interior life. His dialogues, written when he was a catechumen, sought to know "God and the soul" by the use of reason. Twenty years later, his goal remained, but a remarkable change had occurred in his method. His sermons as a bishop exhorted his hearers: "You would see God? God is love."[23]

In what follows, I explore St. Augustine's emerging understanding of "God is love" as discussed in his earliest (extant) treatise, *De beata uita* (*beata u.* 386 CE), his Easter sermons on First John (415 CE), and *Enchiridion* (*ench.* 421 CE). In old age his multiple complaints of physical weariness and weakness, and his longing for undisturbed time, reveal his awareness that his life on earth was drawing to a close, making his increased desire for meditation compelling.

ST. AUGUSTINE'S DISCURSIVE FIELDS

Readers who seek to understand Augustine at a deeper than superficial level should not assume that interests and understandings occurring at different times in his life have identical meaning. Almost inevitably, an author's interests, knowledge, methods, values, and "fields of stabilization" change—subtly or dramatically—across time. Arnold Davidson has defined a field of stabilization as a "determinate conceptual space" (historical, rhetorical, philosophical), *within which* statements "come to be comprehensible."[24] In other words, a word, a phrase, or an idea takes its denotative meaning, its connotations, and its "emotional coloration"[25] from a "set of concepts and the way they fit together."[26] The same word or concept, in different fields of stabilization, *means* differently. Even verbal identity

---

22. *Io. eu. tr.* 17.11.
23. *Ep. Io. tr.* 7.10; trans. Burnaby, *Ten Homilies*, 317.
24. Davidson, *Emergence*, 136.
25. Carruthers, *Craft of Thought*, 53–54.
26. Davidson, *Emergence*, 127.

can hide "radically different concepts."[27] Thus, one must compare "not words or isolated formulas, but whole conceptual structures; otherwise our comparisons will be misleading, indeed pointless."[28]

In order to notice the striking extent to which Augustine's understanding of God's love changed in the different occasions and situations in which he spoke and wrote, the following two sections sketch Augustine's understanding of "God and the soul" thirty years apart, first at the beginning of his life as a Christian in a philosophical retreat; second, as a Christian bishop, student of Scripture, and preacher. In both his earliest dialogues and in his mature sermons and letters, he fervently sought to "see God." But the method and content of his search changed dramatically.

Cassiciacum 386 CE

Augustine's *Confessions* describes his conversion to philosophy at the age of nineteen. As he was reading Cicero's *Hortensius* (a work now lost), Cicero's "exhortation to philosophy" filled him with "a burning desire for the immortality of wisdom," altering "my way of *feeling*."

> I was on fire then, my God, I was on fire to leave earthly things behind and fly back to you . . . that book inflamed me with the love of wisdom. . . . I was urged on and inflamed with a passionate zeal to love and seek and obtain and embrace and hold fast wisdom itself, whatever it might be.[29]

Cicero attracted him to wisdom but offered no instruction in how to approach wisdom. Augustine reports that he immediately filled in the content of Cicero's exhortation: "for with you [God] is wisdom." In retrospect he interpreted the experience as effectively "turning my prayers to you, Lord, and [giving] me different ambitions and desires." Augustine supplied the link to the God he had

---

27. Davidson, *Emergence*, 140.
28. Davidson, *Emergence*, 138.
29. *Conf.* 3.4.7; trans. Warner, *Confessions*, 57.

"imbibed with his mother's milk." The rest, as they say, is history. Beginning in those unforgettable moments as a teenager, Augustine began to integrate his conversion to philosophy with Christianity, a complex process in that he sought not only to switch from one loyalty to another, but also to retrieve what continued to be useful from his philosophical and rhetorical training. He began with study of Scripture, which he initially found "unworthy of comparison with the grand style of Cicero."[30] However, after intensive study Augustine understood Scripture as the language of his interior life, as well as the language of his public ministry.

Shortly after his conversion to celibacy, but before his baptism (Easter, 387 CE), Augustine organized a retreat in a spacious villa at Cassiciacum with several friends, his son, Adeodatus, and his mother, Monica. The gathering was to be a philosophical exploration, conducted in *otium*, leisure. *Otium* was a highly respected and eagerly sought condition among educated men in classical and late antiquity. It required withdrawal from the usual exigencies of living, but *otium* was not a vacation; it was, rather, freedom for uninterrupted conversation with earnest interlocutors. The goal was vigorous exercise of the participants' rational capacity for the purpose of seeking truth embedded in words and concepts.

At Cassiciacum Augustine wrote philosophical dialogues. Presumably the real conversations he was engaged in prompted and inspired him, but Augustine both posed questions and responded to them. Both "R" (Reason) and "A" (Augustine) were characters in his mind. *Beata u.* explored what is needed to produce "the happy life." In this early treatise Augustine declared that he valued faith over reason, but his loyalty to reason is evident in both the subject matter and method of the Cassiciacum dialogues: "reason is the gaze of the soul," and "virtue is correct and proper reason."[31]

Augustine declared his intention for the conversations. He sought to know "God and the soul, neither of which I know."[32] Beginning with a litany of invocations, Augustine addressed God,

30. *Conf.* 3.5.9.
31. *Sol.* 1.6.13.
32. *Sol.* 1.2.7.

"whom everything loves which is capable of loving whether knowingly or unknowingly."[33] "R" asks whether he loves his friends; "A" replies that he loves them because they have rational souls, and he loves them more "the better use they make of the rational soul."[34] He knows his friends, he said, through his intellect; their rational souls "can be known in no other way."[35] Asked whether he has overcome lust, "A" replied, "There is nothing I should avoid so much as marriage . . . it is with dread (*horror*) and disgust or boredom (*taedium*) that I even recall it."[36] Pressed further, however, he acknowledged that he might consider marrying a wealthy woman who could support his *otium*, a relationship, he said that would *not* be "something to be cherished," but rather, "something to be tolerated."[37]

In Augustine's time and place, it was unusual to include a woman in a philosophical retreat.[38] Describing the occasion a decade later, Augustine as much as acknowledged that his mother was brought along to cook and clean for the company: "She gave to each one of us the care a mother gives to her son, and to each one of us the service which a daughter gives to her father."[39] Monica also observed the conversations, however, and the friends must have been startled when she suddenly "woke up" (*euigilans*) and interrupted the discussion. At the moment, the group was discussing "God, the true measure," and they admitted, "we have not yet reached our measure . . . we are not yet wise and happy." Monica interjected, "This is undoubtedly the happy life, that is, the perfect life which we must assume that we can attain soon by a well-founded faith, a joyful hope, and an ardent love."[40] Her observation

33. *Sol.* 1.1.2.
34. *Sol.* 1.2.7.
35. *Sol.* 1.3.8.
36. *Sol.* 1.10.17.
37. *Sol.* 1.11.19.

38. There are earlier examples of women's participation in Greek philosophical dialogues, and there were female monasteries led by women (one of whom was Augustine's sister).

39. *Conf.* 9.9.
40. *Beata u.* 35; trans. Schopp, *Happy Life*, 83.

played an unexpectedly strong role, both at the time, and in Augustine's future thought.

Faith, hope, and love are not philosophical virtues, but reminded of them, Augustine, writing several weeks later, began to explore their philosophical content. He wrote that faith believes that the vision they seek will bring happiness; hope trusts that it will see the desired vision if it seeks intently; and love longs to see. Augustine concludes that these exercises will produce the vision of God, that is, "reason arriving at its goal."[41] Many years later, in another discursive field, faith, hope, and love will ground St. Augustine's summation of Christian faith in his *ench*.

Scholars have disagreed on whether Augustine was a philosopher or a Christian at Cassiciacum. Clearly, he was both. He was thinking philosophically, asking philosophical questions and reasoning in the self-conscious format of a philosophical inquiry. But he was also *beginning* a long process of converting to the language of Scripture and the Christian church. Cassiciacum was a first step in his gradual replacement of the language, method, values, and goal of philosophy, the beginning of a series of conversions too intimately and fundamentally life-changing to occur instantly. Augustine's voluminous publications permit his readers to trace the transformation of his fundamental allegiances, even as he retrieved the aspects of his youthful study of philosophy and rhetoric that he found valuable in his new discursive field. Augustine often described his meditation, from his days as a catechumen until very close to his death, but the discursive field within which his ideas and practices received meaning changed from his Cassiciacum dialogues until it was stabilized in Scripture and the Christian church.

---

41. *Sol.* 1.6.13; 1.7.14.

Hippo, 415 CE

> First see if you yet know how to love yourself. . . . But if you have not learned to love yourself, I am afraid that you are likely to cheat your neighbor as yourself.[42]

The field of stabilization within which St. Augustine spoke for the rest of his life was the Christian church. He had been engaged for almost three decades in an intensive study of Scripture when he preached on the First Epistle of John at Eastertide 415 CE. His seventh homily retrieved a phrase from his Cassiciacum *Soliloquies* but the statement, "anyone who loves, loves God, knowingly or unknowingly," *meant differently* in its present situation. The statement appears now in a sermon, preached by a Christian bishop, its truth validated by a different authority than reason: "From the gospels and the apostles we hear 'God is love.'"[43] Augustine interpreted its meaning, not only within scriptural authority, but also within a Catholic church that had emerged from the fourth-century ecumenical councils with articulated creeds and standardized practices. Even what it is to "know" had changed. No longer the result of a reasoning process, Augustine said that it is appropriate for Christians to say "we *know* what we believe."[44]

Moreover, Augustine often remarked that he learned by his own experience.[45] His hermeneutical practice was to use the lens of his experience to understand Scripture—and to bring Scripture to interrogate and illuminate his experience. Readers observe him *thinking* in scriptural language, and his publications and sermons weave scriptural phrases together with his reflections. As a Christian, he "silently thought"[46]—assumed—that the truth of his inner

---

42. S. 128.3.5, trans. Hill, *Sermons* III/4, 295; *ciu.* 10.3.2; trans. Dyson, *City of God*, 395.

43. *Ep. Io. tr* .9.9.

44. *Retr.* 1.14.3: "When we speak in common usage, we know both what we perceive through the bodily senses and what we believe on the authority of trustworthy witnesses" (trans. Bogan, *Retractions*, 60–61).

45. *Conf.* 8.5.

46. The phrase is Michel Foucault's, referring to unexamined assumptions that influence thought and action.

experience and the truths of Scripture were never in conflict; he believed that they could always be trusted to reflect and interpret one another.[47]

In this discursive field, Augustine's homilies on First John show a converted understanding of love, based on his many years of experience and intensive study of Scripture.

> Does it then follow that he who loves his brother loves God also? Of necessity he must love God: of necessity he must love love itself. He cannot love his brother and not love love: he cannot help loving love. And if he loves love, he needs must love God: in loving love he is loving God.... If God is love, whoever loves love, loves God.[48]

This cluster of close reasoning (*pace* Cassiciacum) became the basis of Augustine's further reflections on love. A few years later (421 CE), his summary of essential Christian beliefs further extended his claim for the power of love:

> The greater the measure in which love dwells in a person, the better is the person in whom it dwells. For when there is a question as to whether a person is good, one does not ask what he believes, or what he hopes, but what he loves.[49]

For a champion of orthodox doctrine, this is a remarkable statement! Wait, what? It doesn't matter what a person *believes*, but only her capacity for loving? Well, no, Augustine will not go that far, for he goes on to say that "the one who loves *the right object* will also believe and hope rightly."[50] Nevertheless, he has come a long way from needing to be reminded that faith, hope, and love are essential for "the happy life"—a goal of reason that he no longer sought.

Augustine notes that "the apostle" declares love to be *greater* than faith and hope (1 Cor 13:13). But he goes beyond saying that

---

47. *Ep.* 216, 6.

48. *Ep. Io. tr.* 9.10; trans. Burnaby, *Homilies*, 336.

49. *Ench.* 31.117, trans. Peebles, *Faith, Hope, and Charity*, 467.

50. *Ench.* 31.117, trans. Peebles, *Faith, Hope, and Charity*, 467 (emphasis added).

love is greater than faith or hope. He describes the vast power of love *either* to *dissolve* or to *absorb* other energies. He did not say so directly, but it seems safe to infer that he had learned from his "own experience" that love dissolves lust, "carrying over" the energy, the formerly tyrannizing "weight" of lust, into love. His overwhelming sense of loss when his longtime partner was "torn from [his] side (*conf*. 6.15) implicitly acknowledges such a transformation. "Carnal lust reigns where there is not the love of God."[51] But love melts lust without residue. "Lust diminishes as love grows, till the latter grows to such a height that it can grow no higher."[52] Augustine knew from his own experience that a relationship which began as a sexual agreement (*pactum libinosi*) can evolve into love.[53]

Like lust, fear is also dissolved by love. In his mature writings on meditation, Augustine consistently described fear as both motivation and energy for meditation. However, his later writings acknowledge that fear is temporarily useful, but ultimately it is overwhelmed by love: Fear "prepares the place for love, but when love has taken up its dwelling, the fear that had created space for love is expelled."[54] He used the same formula for the dissolution of fear as for lust: as one expands, the other diminishes; "the greater the love, the less the fear." One of his last sermons repeats this powerful claim: "Fear should grow less the closer we approach to our home country, and those who are arriving will have none at all. What has put fear out the door . . . is the love of God, whom you are loving with your whole heart and with your whole soul and with your whole mind."[55]

Love not only has power to dissolve lust and fear, it also assimilates into itself a virtue that Augustine valued very highly, namely humility: "All Christians should hold fast to humility because they derive their name Christians from Christ; and no person who studies his gospel carefully fails to find him the teacher

---

51. *Ench*. 118.
52. *Ench*. 32.121.
53. *Conf*. 4.2.2.
54. *Ep. Io. tr*. 9.4.
55. *S*. 348.2.

of humility."[56] His treatise, *De sancta uirginitate* (*uirg.*, 401 CE), expressed his anxiety that one who has received the great gift of virginity—"the chosen among the chosen" (*in electus electius*)—could lose its reward through pride, the furtive enemy of humility. Toward the close of the treatise, Augustine realized: "At this point someone will say, 'This is no longer a treatise on virginity, but on humility'" (*uirg.* 52). But *caritas* absorbs humility into itself: "Love is the guardian of humility, and God is love. . . . If you love him who is meek and humble of heart, I have no fear of any pride in you."[57] Augustine concluded, "it is idle to worry that humility may be lacking where there is glowing love."[58]

Augustine stated at Cassiciacum that God is love, but his knowledge was abstract, not experiential. The concept's "collapse into immediacy"[59] was not the result of a single moment of insight, but rather, of his long practice of meditation. His study of First John led him to suggest that God-is-love is "all you need to know":

> God is love. . . . If nothing else were said in praise of love in all the passages of this epistle, nothing else whatsoever in any other page of Scripture, and this were the one and only thing we heard from the voice of God's spirit—for God is love—we should ask for nothing more.[60]

At Cassiacum Augustine identified his mind and its ability to discern truth through reason as the only access to knowing God. A decade later, when he wrote *Confessions*, his self-identity had altered fundamentally: "my weight is my love; by it I am carried wherever I am carried."[61] "Weight" is more than a metaphor in this statement. Love, "a stronger form of will,"[62] is an incorporeal but

56. *Uirg.* 33.
57. *Uirg.* 56.
58. *Uirg.* 54.
59. The phrase is R. G. Collingwood's, used frequently in *The Idea of History*, referring to suddenly "hearing in the heart" something that has hitherto been known abstractly.
60. *Ep. Io. tr.* 7.4; trans. Burnaby, *Homilies*, 314.
61. *Conf.* 13.9.
62. *Trin.* 15.21.

nevertheless *substantial* "weight" that stabilizes the psyche, calming its erratic and insatiable attraction to myriad objects in the desperate fear that something will be missed. Pride is also "weighty," but pride's weight is an undertow, a counter-weight that drags the psyche "out and away by the voices of my own error."[63]

THE OLD AUGUSTINE AND DOCTRINE

St. Augustine's request (424 CE) for uninterrupted time for study decisively shows that he longed for time for prayer, study, reminiscence, and thought. But his last quarrel with Julian of Eclanum demonstrates no effort at economy of speech; quite the opposite, readers have seldom seen St. Augustine so garrulous! In this section, I do not explore the details of the argument; rather I seek to understand *what lay beneath* the old Augustine's reasoning on matters of doctrine, to what values he was loyal—values that still prompted his participation in "long-winded" argument while simultaneously compelling him to seek time for meditation.

Because Augustine had a pervasive and lasting influence on Christian doctrine, it is often assumed that doctrine was the dominating interest of his Christian life. The treatises, letters, and sermons of his last decade tell a different story. His late writings still demonstrate responsible efforts to respond to the challenges and questions addressed to him as a bishop, but his weariness in his final years is evident in a lack of zest; he was tired of arguing. Readers notice repetitiousness in these writings; Augustine also complained of repetition, expressing impatience with questions he had already painstakingly discussed.[64] Moreover, his *feeling* of what was essential had altered.

The extent to which Augustine valued feeling over intellectual understanding is not often recognized in studies of his thought. In

---

63. *Conf.* 4.15.

64. Lack of libraries and interlibrary loans in Augustine's time meant that anyone who wanted to read a treatise or sermon of Augustine's went directly to him to request it.

Beautiful Bodies

his usage, "feeling" (singular) is not identical with emotions, or even with feelings (plural).

> Augustine used the word "feeling" (*adfectus*) to describe a cluster of intellect, emotions, and body. Feeling collects and expresses desire, belief, perceptions of beauty, regret, gratitude, delight, and more. Rationality is *part* of "feeling," but is neither dominant nor decisive.... *Feeling gathers, reveals, and directs the deep longing of the whole person.*[65]

Everyday usage does not help to express this very significant distinction. *Conf.* narrates multiple examples of Augustine's and others' experience of scriptural phrases that suddenly "collapsed into immediacy," taking flame in the hearer, eradicating doubt, and energizing immediate and lasting decision. Augustine's conversion to celibacy, prompted by St. Anthony's exemplary conversion, included a Scripture verse (Rom 13:13-14) that "sprang to my mind from the depths of my heart."[66] "You were inside me, deeper than the deepest recesses of my heart."[67] This, *this* is the "place," Augustine wrote, in which "God does something in us . . . that is easy to feel and impossible to explain."[68]

> Augustine identified the kind of hearer to whom he preached: Give me a lover, and that one perceives what I am saying. Give me one who desires, one who hungers, give me one who wanders in this exile and thirsts, one

---

65. Miles, *Reading Augustine*, 2 (emphasis added). Augustine's word for reason is *animus*, frequently (but misleadingly) translated "mind" (presumed to indicate intellect alone). According to *Cassell's Latin Dictionary*, however, the first meaning of *animus* is "the spiritual or rational principle of life, *the seat of feeling, the heart.*" A long argument that cannot be attempted here would be necessary to propose that Augustine's discussion of "will" in *Confessions* 8 suggests that strongly conflicting "wills" are not primarily a conflict of ideas, but an impasse of conflicting *feelings.*

66. *Conf.* 4.13. The verse that penetrated to the core of the wealthy St. Anthony's resistance was "Sell all that you have and give to the poor." Augustine's conversion to celibacy was similarly directed to his strongest resistance: "Make no provision for the flesh, to gratify its desires" (*conf.* 8.12).

67. *Conf.* 3.6.
68. *Io. eu. tr.* 40.5.

who sighs for the fountain of the eternal homeland, give me such a one and that one knows what I say. But if I speak to one whose heart is cold, that one is ignorant of what I am saying.[69]

Augustine's high esteem for feeling *ex intimo corde meo*, influenced his understanding of doctrine. Significantly, the doctrines that he found "inscrutable," "humanly incomprehensible," and "better left to God," are those that do not produce a strong feeling, that do not resonate *intus*, in the hearer's or reader's heart. Acknowledging the limit of his ability to comprehend "God's ways" by examining Scripture in the light of his own experience—and his experience in the light of Scripture—Augustine recognized that some questions are better left to God, that is, *in abstraction*. Two of the doctrines he puzzled over in his last years—namely, predestination and perseverance—are not experiential: Why are predestination and perseverance given to some and not to others? "God's ways, both in mercy and judgment, are past finding out.... Let us not endeavor to look into that which is inscrutable."[70] At the close of his life, he said of inscrutable doctrines, "I did not know then, and I still do not know."[71]

Do doctrines that must be believed rather than understood from one's experience carry a feeling? They do, perhaps not directly, but as an effect; that feeling is humility.[72] Augustine feared that the slightest acknowledgment of human merit or initiative inevitably invites incursions of pride, the lurking enemy of grace. For Augustine, humility is a sufficient and ample benefit of belief in doctrines "best left to God." The young Augustine had been distressed that Scripture taught that God, in Jesus, appeared in a human body, fundamentally—he thought at the time—compromising divinity.[73]

---

69. *Io. eu. tr.* 26.4; trans. is my own.
70. *Perseu.* 11.25.
71. *Retr.* I.1.3.
72. St. Thomas Aquinas implied that the experience of grace carried a feeling: "Grace is a glow of soul, a real quality, like beauty of body." *Summa* 1a–2ae, Q. 1102, art. 2; trans. Fairweather, *Aquinas on Nature*, 159.
73. *Conf.* 7.17.

Beautiful Bodies

He learned humility from the humble Jesus.[74] For Augustine, the primary significance and "lasting importance of Jesus was not his miraculous birth, nor his teachings, nor his raising the dead to life"—it was his humility in accepting a human body.[75]

Monks at Hadrumetum accused Augustine's doctrine of grace of nullifying human free will. They proposed that a person's initial turn to God is a matter of human will. Augustine replied that *both* human free will and God's grace are essential. He affirmed both without specifying the proportion or role of each: "For these things are both commanded us and are shown to be God's gifts in order that we may understand both that we do them and that God makes us do them. . . . There is both free will in man and grace from God."[76] In short, the doctrines of predestination and perseverance must remain abstract, that is, left to God.

The doctrine of original sin is different. Augustine intensified the doctrine beyond its earlier understanding as a debilitating lack or flaw in human nature.[77] "My personal experience enabled me to understand what I had read, that the flesh lusts against the spirit, and the spirit against the flesh" (Gal 5:17). Augustine characterized his youthful experience of intractable and domineering sexual lust as a "hard chain," an irresistible "habit," "slavery."[78] *Based on his experience*, he asserted that *concupiscentia* is one consequence of a well-nigh universally experienced *feeling*, namely, sexual lust.

Largely because of the vividness with which he described his experience, many of Augustine's interpreters have ignored his awareness of the limitations of his first hermeneutic principle, namely, the convergence of Scripture and his "own experience." Although the doctrine of original sin helped Augustine to understand his experience, he also understood that original sin is

---

74. *Conf.* 7.9, 13, 7.18, 24, 7.20.26.

75. Miles, *Reading Augustine*, 8.

76. *Ep.* 214.

77. Williams, *Ideas of the Fall*. The doctrine of original sin had a long history before Augustine. Tertullian had described original sin as *uitium originalis*, original weakness.

78. *Conf.* 8.6.13.

neither caused by, nor coterminous with, sexual lust. "Augustine did not understand the primal sin as carnal . . . original sin has no 'efficient' cause, only a 'deficient' cause," namely, that human beings were created *ex nihilo*.[79] The effects of original sin are multiple: death and susceptibility to disease and weakness; also, "we have lost much of our beauty, [we] cannot reason clearly enough to understand ourselves, and are often dis-unified in mind, finding many desires or thoughts at odds with others."[80]

Even in old age,[81] Augustine said, we do not outlive the human condition in which "the flesh lusts against the spirit and the spirit against the flesh."[82]

> So long as we are living here, brothers and sisters, that is how it is; that's how it is even for us who have grown old in this warfare; sure, we have fewer and lesser enemies, but we still have them, nonetheless. Our enemies too have to some extent got worn out by age, but even so, tired though they may be, they never stop disturbing the quiet of old age with all sorts of impulses. The battle is fiercer for young people; we know all about that, we've been through it too.[83]

Although Augustine's experience helped him to understand the ineluctable grip of original sin, he recognized that sexual lust does not "explain" the doctrine. *Concupiscentia* is merely one of its consequences.

---

79. Couenhoven, "St. Augustine's Doctrine," 366. On the many forms of *concupiscentia*, including "good *concupiscentia*," see also Gerald Bonner's "Libido and Concupiscentia," 359–96.

80. Couenhoven, "St. Augustine's Doctrine," 382.

81. Edmond Hill OP notes that Augustine would have been about sixty when he said this—old age according to his contemporary standards; Hill, *Sermons* III/4, 302 n. 17.

82. *S.* 128.11; trans. Hill, *Sermons* III/4, 299.

83. In this volume the translator consistently translates "fratres" as "brothers and sisters," a translation about which I am ambivalent. On the one hand, Augustine is presumably preaching to a congregation of both sexes; on the other, a translation that may ring better in contemporary ears may obscure the historical as well as the textual address to "fratres." See also *ciu.* 18.4.

In his later writings Augustine emphasized the *physicality* of original sin. In debate with Julian of Eclanum he said that original sin is transmitted from Adam's (physical) *seed* at the moment of conception. He hypothesized that *before* original sin, conception would have occurred by the rational choice of the will.[84] Presently however, he said, conception cannot happen if it lacks "wholly evil" *concupiscentia*.[85] St. Augustine was more confident interpreting and defending doctrines that he *felt*, or *had* felt.[86]

Augustine's last interlocutor, Julian of Eclanum (exiled in CE 418 for Pelagian beliefs), called to Augustine's attention several complications, even apparent contradictions, in his doctrine of original sin. Tacitly referencing the principle that doctrines should be examined for how they *act*—what they *produce*—Julian suggested that the doctrine of original sin promotes immorality: "Because you blame defects of character on the filth of nature . . . no one needs to try to change."[87] He argued further that original sin, inherent in every human being, necessarily reveals a fundamental flaw in human nature, implying the creator's responsibility: "Whatever is attributed to necessity strikes at the creator."[88] Moreover, belief in individual predestination, occurring "before the foundations of the world," Julian said, inevitably raises concerns about God's justice.

---

84. *Ciu.* 14.23; trans. Dyson, *City of God*, 623.

85. *Nupt. et conc.* 1.1.1; trans. Huegelmeyer, *Adulterous Marriages*. Augustine universalized male sexual experience, not acknowledging that women do not *necessarily* experience lust in conceiving. Thus, Jesus's conception and virgin birth, believed to have occurred without male lust, did not transmit original sin to Jesus. Julian argued that Jesus, if he was fully human, would have inherited original sin.

86. Michel Foucault's *Confessions of the Flesh*, vol. 4, describes St. Augustine's understanding of sexuality in the context of his Christian predecessors and contemporaries. May 4–June 3, 2021, Rice University sponsored a series of reviews by Augustine scholars Peter Brown, Mark Jordan, Elizabeth Clark, and others. The Zoom series, "Foucault's Confessions," insightfully addressed the strengths and weaknesses of Foucault's arguments in *Confessions of the Flesh*.

87. *C. Iul. opus imperf.* 26.

88. *C. Iul. opus imperf.* 2.15; trans. O'Donnell, Augustine, 370.

More fundamentally, Julian challenged not only Augustine's *belief* but also the *experience* that grounded his reinterpretation of original sin, or at least, his "laundered memories."[89] Perhaps Julian's sexual experience differed in dramatic intensity from Augustine's. If so, *both St. Augustine and Julian universalized their experience.* Julian believed that God created sex, both for human pleasure and—obviously—for the perpetuation of the human race.[90] At Cassiciacum, Augustine remembered sexual experience with "dread and disgust."[91] Of course, his adamant protest should be seen as occurring within the discursive field in which he participated at the time, in which reason was privileged as both the method and the goal of knowledge.[92] Nevertheless, a decade later when he wrote *Confessions* Augustine still acknowledged no pleasure in sexual experience.

Clearly, in the last decade of his life, Augustine was not uninterested in doctrine. He simply found other aspects of his experience of God more essential, more fundamental. He no longer relished intellectual debate, so he sought to end arguments as quickly as possible, yet insisting on his understanding. Nothing in his theological world encouraged him to "agree to disagree" with what he considered heresy.

AUGUSTINE'S MEDITATION

I cannot even comprehend myself whom you have made; And yet in my meditation a fire flames out, so that I seek your face evermore.[93]

Throughout St. Augustine's Christian life, meditation informed his self-knowledge as well as his public life as preacher and teacher,

89. Carruthers, *Craft*, 175.
90. *C. Iul. opus imperf.* 29.
91. *Sol.* 1.10.17.
92. Robinson, *Body*, 31: "Body" ($\sigma\varpi\mu\alpha$), God's good creation, is not "flesh" ($\sigma\alpha\rho\xi$), Paul's designation for the whole person under sin's agenda.
93. *Trin.* 15.7.13; trans. McKenna, *St. Augustine*, 469.

but in his last days, meditation became essential to him. As discussed earlier, Augustine's meditation involved several exercises, study of Scripture, prayer, and his memories which, considered in retrospect, revealed God's leading. Memories are created by feeling; an event or moment is remembered when it carries strong feeling; if it does not, it is not remembered. The external circumstances in which strongly felt experience occurs merely house the memory. Remarkably, Augustine's *theme* was God's ubiquitous leading *within* the apparently scattershot choices and events of his life, in "the bad and the good that I did" (*malis et bonus meis; retr.* 2.6.1). *God's leading excluded none of his experience.*[94]

Memories of his life were his access to knowing himself. "I *am* my memories," he wrote. "Great indeed is the power of memory! It is something terrifying, my God, a profound and infinite multiplicity, and *this thing is I myself.*"[95] God was not to be found *in* his memory, in himself, but it was his memories which provoked his momentary startled touch (*ictu cordis*) of "that which is."[96] "I will go past this force of mine called memory. . . . I mount up through my memories *toward* you . . . for I desire to reach you at the point *from which* you may be reached."[97] Sensory memories are also essential to Augustine's memories: "Do you not have ears in the heart? . . . Do you not have eyes in the heart? . . . Your heart both sees and hears . . . in your heart you hear with what you see with."[98]

Augustine's readers may wonder why he narrated his youthful transgressions in detail in *Confessions*. I suggest that he did so to illustrate his striking understanding of God's method: "You [God] were dragging me by the force of my own desires" (*et me*

---

94. Augustine's search, related in *Confessions* for God's leading interior to the circumstances and choices of his life, occurred before his preaching on the psalms resulted in his change to communal identity as member of the body of Christ. This profound change in his perspective affected his meditation, but did not alter its necessity as the nourishment of his Christian life and ministry.

95. *Conf.* 10.6.

96. *Conf.* 7.17.

97. *Conf.* 10.17; trans. Warner, *Confessions*, 227.

98. *Io. eu. tr.* 18.10; trans. Hill, *Gospel of John 1–40*, 330–31.

cupiditatis raperes; conf. 5.8). God works *intus,* interior to the choices and circumstances of life:

> God does something in us, I do not know what, in a spiritual, non-material way; it is neither a sound to strike the ears, nor a color to be distinguished by the eyes, nor a smell to be picked up by the nostrils, nor flavor to be judged by the palate, nor something hard or soft to be perceived by touching it; all the same, it is something that is easy to feel and impossible to explain.[99]

Viewed from the outside, Augustine said, we "cannot tell the real meaning of any action."[100] At Cassiciacum, Augustine and his friends had interrogated words in order to identify truths they thought of as above the fray of human life, "Wisdom," timeless and universal, his confessions are an extended meditation and a vivid illustration of his meditation practice. In *Confessions* 7, Augustine illustrated by narrating two different accounts of how he arrived at a decision; one account describes his external influences and conscious choices, while the other demonstrates his awareness (in retrospect) of God's inner direction.[101] Both accounts are true—albeit from different perspectives.

There were intellectual conversions in Augustine's journey, but they were not his primary access to experience of himself and God. Rather, his memories constituted a strongly *emotional* route. Tears, the evidence of strong emotion, invariably accompanied meditation. His sermon on Psalm 6 specifies that meditation requires weeping that penetrates to the innermost part of the heart, tears that do not merely wash (*laudari*) but scour (*rigatio*) the heart.[102] Possidius, Augustine's friend and biographer, reported that on his deathbed Augustine wept "constantly and copiously" (*iugitur ac ubertim*) as he meditated.[103]

---

99. *Io. eu. tr.* 40.5; trans. Hill, *Gospel of John 1–40,* 598–99.
100. *Conf.* 3.9.17.
101. *Conf.* 7.14.20.
102. *En. ps.* 6.7; trans. Boulding, *Expositions of the Psalms,* 108–9.
103. Possidius, *Uita,* 31; my own translation.

ST. AUGUSTINE'S LAST DESIRE

Beauty grows in you with the growth of love, for love itself is the soul's beauty.[104]

St. Augustine's first desire was also his last desire. His longing, articulated at Cassiciacum, was "to know God and the soul."[105] At Cassiciacum, Augustine and his friends had interrogated words in order to identify truths they thought of as above the fray of human life, "Wisdom," timeless and universal. His desire grew throughout his life; nearing the end of his life on earth, it gathered urgency. However, his access to knowing "God and the soul" in his last years was no longer the truth accessible only to reason. Augustine's knowledge of "God and the soul" was the result of his meditation by which he recognized *in his memories,* in him*self,* God's fine-tuned intimate management of his life: "You (God) were inside me, deeper than the deepest recesses of my heart."[106]

His goal of attaining knowledge of God and the soul remained the same, but his method changed during his Christian life. Although he played the authoritative roles of bishop and preacher, *within* the body of Christ, the Christian community, Augustine still longed to be seen, *"in myself."* He knew himself—*intus*—not as the invincible defender of doctrine, authoritative bishop, or prodigious author seen by others. "By loving, you see, we live from the heart."[107] In 429 CE Augustine sent a copy of his *Confessions,* to a "beloved son," Darius; his *Confessions,* he said, "tell what I was in myself . . . not what others say of me."[108] To be seen *in himself*

---

104. *Ep. Io. tr.* 9.9; trans. Burnaby, *Ten Homilies,* 336.

105. *Sol.* 2.7.

106. *Conf.* 3.6. Augustine wrote this statement before his self-identification as communal occurred in the first decades of the fifth century. Augustine's two identities are not necessarily successive; they are compatible and mutually enhancing. The individual is not erased but fulfilled within Christian community.

107. *Io. eu. tr.* 2.11; also *Io. eu. tr.* 25.15: "the proud throw away their inwardness; the humble seek the things within."

108. *Ep.* 231.6; trans. Parsons, *St. Augustine,* 163.

St. Augustine's Last Desire

was to be seen in his longing and vulnerability; he repeated "pray for me" five times in this letter. He also asked for prayer in other correspondence: "I ask you to pray for me wholeheartedly and constantly" (*instanter et uigilanter*), he wrote.[109]

St. Augustine's self knowledge did not exclude his experience of lifelong subjective conflict between flesh and spirit. The truth Augustine learned to seek in meditation was *the truth of his own life*, that is, God's leading *within* the chaos and pain of his desires. In his long practice of meditation, Augustine found strength that both incorporates and transcends truth, namely, love: "The victory of truth is love."[110] As he moved away from seeking abstract truths accessed by reason, meditation replaced reasoning; experience outweighed abstraction; love transcended intellectual knowledge.

Augustine realized that a vision of a God *above* the vicissitudes of human life is not achievable in this life. Knowing God is not the result of impeccable reasoning, but is, rather, a long process of walking the walk. "One is not only instructed so as to see you . . . but also so as to grow strong enough so as to lay hold on you, and one who cannot see you for the distance, may yet walk along the road by which he will arrive and see you and lay hold on you."[111] Augustine advised his congregation not to take his metaphor literally: "we go to him not by walking, but by loving."[112]

Yet God *can* be seen in this life. "If you would see God . . . God is love."

> In terms of precept, the love of God comes first; but in terms of practice, the love of neighbor comes first. . . . Because you do not yet see God, you will deserve to see him by loving your neighbor, for by loving your neighbor, you cleanse your eye for seeing God.[113]

---

109. *Ep.* 215; trans. Parsons, *St. Augustine*, 62.
110. *S.* 358.1; trans. Hill, *Sermons* III/10, 190.
111. *Conf.* 7.21.27; trans. Warner, *Confessions*, 158.
112. *Ep.* 155.4.13; trans. Parsons, *St. Augustine*, 315.
113. *Io. eu. tr.* 5.10; 17.8; trans. Hill, *Gospel of John 1–40*, 312.

Beautiful Bodies

Seeing God is not accomplished by reasoning in disengagement from the urgencies and cares of life. "Let us seek God with our hands; let not works cease.... Let there be no idle yearning."[114] Love is bodied: "Love has feet, which take us to the church, love has hands which give to the poor, love has eyes ... love has ears."[115] Uninterrupted time for meditation was essential to St. Augustine's experience of God, but the *otium* of the philosopher had become the *otium sanctum* of the monk in meditation: time set apart for prayer, gathering and reconsidering his life, and attentiveness to God *ex intimo corde meo*.

"God is love" is not an abstract truth, nor a concept: "Any one who thinks of God as anything other than life itself [*uitam ipsam*] has an absurd notion of God."[116] But even "life itself" is an abstraction until it "collapses into immediacy," as *one's own life*—Augustine's life, in its detail and particularity. In Augustine's meditation, "life itself" achieved that immediacy.

St. Augustine identified God in three ways. God is life: "You are the life of souls, the life of lives, the very living life."[117] God is love: "love and you will see God, for God is love."[118] God is beauty, "so old and so new,[119] "the beauty of all things beautiful."[120] Like humility, beauty is a permanent characteristic of God-is-love. Not only do these attributes identify something essential about God, but each acts as a road to seeing God's beauty as interior to the world and the self. According to Augustine, each of these qualities—life, love, and beauty—are *links* that *participate simultaneously* in the world of the senses and the spiritual world, links which do not bridge two separate entities, but disclose that spirit and matter are one world.[121]

---

114. *En. ps.* 76.4 trans. Boulding, *Expositions of the Psalms*, 77.
115. *Ep. Io.tr.* 7, 10; trans. Burnaby, *Ten Homilies*, 317.
116. *Doct. chr.* 1.8.8; trans. Robertson, *On Christian Doctrine*, 12.
117. *Conf.* 3.6.10; trans. Warner, *Confessions*, 59.
118. *Ep. Io. tr.* 7.10; trans. Burnaby, *Ten Homilies*, 317.
119. *Conf.* 10.27.38; trans. Warner, *Confessions*, 235.
120. *Conf.* 3.6.10; trans. Warner, *Confessions*, 59.
121. "We are responsible for what we learn how to see" (Haraway, "Persistence of Vision," in *Writing on the Body*, 289).

St. Augustine's Last Desire

It was *with* his own life, his *feeling* at different moments, minutely remembered, deeply understood, and with profoundly felt gratitude that St. Augustine sought to gather himself to embark upon the greater life, "life itself." As he lay dying, he longed for solitude for meditation in which he could *see* the beauty of his inner life and *feel* the love by which he was led.

Centerpiece

Breathing Together

THE YOUNG AUGUSTINE, PROTAGONIST of his *Confessions*, is the Augustine often encountered for the first time by college students in literature or religion courses. In journalism, as in college classes, this Augustine is usually considered the essential Augustine. The narrative of a young North African who lived over 1,500 years ago, feverish with desire for sex and wisdom is, to be sure, endlessly fascinating. Moreover, many twenty-first-century Western readers detect resemblances to ourselves that encourage us to think we understand him. Yet Augustine did not seek to attract readers, but rather, to "take pleasure in praising his God."[1] He "confessed" most rigorously and continuously to the suffocating *weight* of his longings, emotional, intellectual, social, and spiritual. He described his youthful self as "dragged by my own errors and the weight of my pride."[2] Yet Augustine startlingly characterized God as acting *within* his own desires, even intensifying those desires, to make Augustine weary of his cravings: "You [God] were dragging me by the force of my own desires *in order that these desires might be*

---

1. *Conf.* 1.
2. *Conf.* 4.15.

brought to an end."[3] Many years later, looking back over his life, pondering "the bad and the good that I did" (*malis et bonus meis*; *retr.* 2.6.1), Augustine wrote:

> For such as love God in this way he makes all things work together for good, absolutely all things, even to the extent that if some of them swerve and stray from the path, he makes their very wanderings contribute to their good, because they come back wiser and more humble.[4]

Augustine's *Confessions* is an extended meditation, written when he was about forty years old, in which he recalled and revisited the circumstances and feelings of his childhood and youth, seeking to identify God's leading within both external and subjective events. He described his conversion to God's service as a long *process* of multiple conversions, which began in infancy as he imbibed the name of Christ with his Christian mother's milk.[5] He was, he wrote, "already a Christian" when he faced the momentous decision most readers consider his "conversion," namely, whether to sacrifice "marriage and worldly success" in order to enter a celibate career in God's service. In fact, a series of "conversions" preceded and followed his conversion to celibacy.[6] When he wrote *Confessions*, Augustine identified himself as the product of God's activity in converting and shaping him.

However, Augustine's self-examination in *Confessions* placed him in danger of being "stuck in the past, that is, in the self," in danger of "becoming solipsistic."[7] In his book, *Augustine on Memory*, Kevin Grove traces a major mid-life revision of Augustine's self identity prompted by, and explored in, his sermons on the psalms.[8] These sermons relocate Christian experience, not

3. *Conf.* 5.8 (emphasis added).
4. *Corrept.* 24; 426–27 CE.
5. *Conf.* 1.6; 3.4.
6. *Conf.* 8.8–12 describes Augustine's conversion to celibacy. See Miles, *Reading Augustine*, chapter 3, "Augustine's Conversions," 33–53.
7. Grove, *Augustine on Memory*, 142–43, 220.
8. Grove, *Augustine on Memory*, 4: Augustine's sermons on the psalms was his longest work, "both in years to complete and in number of words

primarily within the individual self, but within the "whole Christ," a "communally constituted" identity "beyond self and interiority."[9] The "whole Christ" configures Christ as head, and the church as body of Christ: "Head and body together form the *totus Christus*, the whole Christ."[10]

In Augustine's mature understanding, the self is no longer primarily the product of God's interior activity, unique to the individual; rather, "the completion of the self is within the whole." Moreover, Augustine and his congregation are "not one person and Christ another. Rather, in the ascended Christ, they are one single individual, head and body."[11] This was to be Augustine's self-identity for the rest of his life. His late writings explain that the "perfect man" is Christ [the Head]; his body is the church: "we being many are one bread, one body."[12] Augustine's eucharistic language is more than metaphoric; it is in the communal *practices* of the church—singing together,[13] praying together, eating and drinking together—that "the body of Christ" is *actualized*. Communal identity does not "minimize individual experience, but connects it to the whole body. . . . [Augustine's] own experience becomes small and lacking in importance compared with the image of Christ which is being communally renewed." The self is not eliminated; rather its isolation is overcome, and "its full resplendence [is] shown within the whole."[14]

. . . beginning shortly after his ordination in 392 and continuing until late in his life."

9. Grove, *Augustine on Memory*, 112.

10. Grove, *Augustine on Memory*, 75.

11. Grove, *Augustine on Memory*, 109.

12. *Ciu.* 22.17–18, 24; trans. Dyson, *City of God*, 1144–46, 1165.

13. Singing together requires breathing together. Singing became, for Augustine, a model of the liturgical practices that create communal identity.

14. Grove, *Augustine on Memory*, 224. Grove's discussion of this crucially important revision of Augustine's self-understanding can be read as an alternative to Peter Brown's interpretation of Augustine's mid-life revision of what he hoped to achieve in this life. In *Augustine of Hippo,* Brown described Augustine's "Lost Future" (chapter 15), as resulting from Augustine's disillusionment with his earlier expectation that "the compulsive force of habit" (142) could be

The colorful and urgently desiring Augustine of the *Confessions* has not disappeared in the mature Augustine. His sermons on the Gospel of John and the First Epistle of John, preached in the second decade of the fifth century, demonstrate that he spoke more personally than ever before in his preaching. Rather than dwelling on tales of his own youthful experience, he foregrounded present experience together, "in the church," as Possidius wrote.[15] He invited his companions in the body of Christ to think with him, to consider whether his interpretation of the Scripture on which he was preaching was both accurate and helpful.

As a former teacher of rhetoric, Augustine knew that a speaker's reference to his relationship with an audience was a well-known and often-practiced rhetorical device. In Augustine's sermons, however, the preacher's self-identity with his congregation was more than rhetorical style; it was theological reality. In sermons, Augustine himself was no longer an object of inquiry and fascination to himself and others, but *a vehicle of connection with his hearers*. He rejected the posture of authority, reminding the congregation frequently that he spoke *with* them as a fellow member of the body of Christ, one who is "becoming Christ" *with* them.

> I beg you, together let us knock; may something come to us to feed us, in accord with that which delights us. Indeed, a great and lovely secret . . . your attention, please, pay close attention and weigh well these words. I will not cast out the one who comes to me. (John 6:37)[16]

---

overcome to enable a life of serene contemplation. Grove argues persuasively that Augustine's mid-life altered expectations should be understood rather as the self, completed within the communally constituted "body of Christ."

15. Possidius, *Uita* 31.9; trans. Weiskotten, *Porphyry*: "I think that those who gained most from him were those who had been able actually to *see and hear him* as he spoke in church" (emphasis added).

16. "Homily 15," trans. Hill, *Gospel of John 1–40*, 442. See chapters 2 and 3 for his "occasional" comments, which I understand as anything but casual; they reminded his hearers of his solidarity with them in "walking on the road."

Beautiful Bodies

A revised humility characterized Augustine's sermons. Still confident of the authority of Scripture and church doctrine, he became less certain of his "voice" as an interpreter of Scripture.

> Be ready to hear the same voice from me as is to be heard from the psalms, a dutiful voice, humble, gentle, not proud, not rowdy, not headstrong, not rash.... So do you want me to tell you things I know? I won't mislead you; listen to what I have believed. Don't let it seem cheap in your eyes, just because you are hearing what I have believed; you are hearing, after all, a genuine confession of faith. If I were to say, though, "listen to what I know," you would be hearing some very rash presumption.... And if any of you, perhaps, can grasp more than I can express, don't waste your time on this thin little trickle, but hurry off to the abundant fountain.[17]

Augustine repeatedly referred in sermons to a *practice* that became popular after Helena, mother of the emperor Constantine, went on pilgrimage to the "Holy Land" in the early fourth century. Augustine proposed that pilgrimage is a metaphor for Christian life. Christians, he wrote, are on the road—*in uia*—toward the "city of God." However, for Augustine, who disliked travel, pilgrimage was not geographical, but spiritual.[18] He explored aspects of geographical pilgrimage that illuminated spiritual pilgrimage. For example, in a literal journey, it was necessary to travel with others for protection and support. So too in a spiritual pilgrimage. Augustine emphasized the importance of trustworthy companions: "Among a certain few there is truth. You now know what it is, if you know among whom it is."[19]

He also frequently used the pilgrimage metaphor "walking," to suggest intentionality, effort, and progress.

---

17. *S.* 362.5 (CE 411); trans. Hill, *Sermons* III/10, 243–44.

18. I have not found any exhortation of Augustine's to his hearers to embark on a geographical pilgrimage. The pilgrimage Augustine advocated was an *interior* pilgrimage: "Do all within"; *Io. eu. tr.* 25.15; trans. Hill, *Gospel of John 1–40*, 442–43.

19. *Util. cred.* 7.16.

> Walk without fear, run, but stay on the road;
> > perhaps you are slightly lame?
> At least do not leave the road; you may take longer,
> > but you will get there.
> Only do not stand still, do not turn back,
> > do not get sidetracked.[20]
>
> Any who find that they have gone astray must return to the road
> > and walk on it, and any who find that they are on the road must
> > go on walking until they arrive.[21]
>
> One is not only instructed so as to see you,
> > but also so as to grow strong enough to hold [*teneat*] you,
> and the one who cannot see you for the distance,
> > may yet walk along the road by which he will arrive
> > and see you and hold you.[22]
>
> Truth speaks interiorly to understanding minds.
> It has aroused us to a great desire for its inner sweetness.
> We seize it by growing, we grow by walking;
> > we walk by making progress so that we may be able to arrive at it.[23]

Augustine corrected his metaphor: "We go to him not by walking, but by loving."[24]

Augustine was keenly interested in the significance of doctrines for the present; he believed that doctrines, supported by Scripture and believed by predecessors in the faith, carried great importance for present belief and practice. The *present* importance of the doctrines of predestination and perseverance, for example, insisted that individuals can do exactly nothing to secure election—by behavior or pleading—but must rather cultivate humility, participating in God's love as a member of Christ's body. Relationships with others are imagined and lived differently in community

---

20. Exposition 2 of Psalm 31, trans. Boulding, *Expositions of the Psalms*, 320.

21. Exposition 2 of Psalm 31, trans. Boulding, *Expositions of the Psalms*, 319–20; also S. 14.6.

22. *Conf.* 7.21, trans. Warner, *Confessions*, 158.

23. *Io eu. tr.* 54.8; trans. Hill, *Gospel of John 41–194*, 175.

24. *Ep.* 155.4; trans. Parsons, *St. Augustine*, 315.

formed and sustained by God's love than as a collection of individuals. In a late letter (429 CE), Augustine addressed Darius, Count of Africa, as "my son, a member of Christ," urging him to "see the feeling in my heart," and urging him to "pray for me; pray, my son, pray. I feel deeply what I am saying."[25] His correspondence demonstrates that Augustine was loved in return. A letter (lacking salutation, but apparently addressed to Augustine) exclaims "Oh! If love could be seen with the eyes! Certainly you would see how much of my love there is in you!"[26]

To participate in the lavish circulation of love of God and neighbor was to breathe the rich air of God's love. It was to sing together—people who sing together, breathe together; to eat and drink together, to pray together, to listen and to ponder together the words of Scripture and sermon together. It was to "become Christ" together.

25. *Ep.* 231.
26. *Ep.* 270.

Chapter Three

How St. Augustine Could Love the God in Whom He Believed

ST. AUGUSTINE, PICTURED BY Western painters holding in his hand his heart blazing with passionate love, consistently and repeatedly insisted—from his earliest writings until close to his death—that the essential characteristic of God is "God is love" (1 John 4:16). Yet he also insisted on the doctrines of original sin and everlasting punishment for the *massa damnata*. This chapter will not explore the rationale or semantics of his arguments, nor the detail and nuance of the doctrines of predestination and perseverance. Rather, I seek to understand, from Augustine's last writings, how he reconciled his strong conviction that God *is* love with doctrines requiring belief in a God who, "before the foundation of the world" (Eph 1:4), determined the fate of individuals to eternal reward or punishment, indifferent to individuals' actions, struggles, or longings. My primary interest is not on Augustine's ability to render these two apparently opposing ideas of God *intellectually* compatible, but rather on his *feeling*, gathered from his last sermons, as he approached death. In brief, how could Augustine love the God in whom he believed?

Beautiful Bodies

INTRODUCTION

It must sometimes be the business of the historian of philosophy to transcribe faithfully the inner contradictions that his philosophic instinct—and admiration—would tempt him to suppress.[1]

After studying St. Augustine for over fifty years, a conspicuous dissonance at the very center of his thought has continued to puzzle me. Augustine's rich prose described God not only as loving but as love itself, intimate and passionate, the source and reality of human love. In a sermon on the First Epistle of John (*ep. Io. tr.*), Augustine quoted 1 John 4:16, "God is love," commenting, and that is all you need to know about God: "For if nothing else were said in praise of love . . . nothing else whatever in any other page of Scripture, and this were the one and only thing we heard from the voice of God's Spirit—'For God is love'—we should ask for nothing more."[2]

Yet Augustine also taught that individuals are the helpless victims of predestination to everlasting reward or punishment. He described a God whose incontrovertible decision has consigned most of the human race, newly born or old in years, to the *massa damnata*, eternally excluded from paradise. The topics of two of his last treatises—predestination and perseverance—appear to nullify human responsibility, leaving people at the mercy of a God who, according to any human standard, is anything but loving. Such a God must inspire fear.

To the question of God's justice, insistently raised by interlocutors,[3] Augustine's strengthened doctrine of original sin allowed him to maintain that God would be perfectly justified in condemning *all* descendants of Adam, the prototypical human being, to everlasting punishment. Having understood this, Augustine's (and his readers') attention can then be focused on gratitude that God's mercy has selected a few to enjoy eternal bliss.

---

1. O'Connell, *St. Augustine's Early Theory*, 152.

2. *Ep. Io. tr.* 7.4; trans. Burnaby, *Ten Homilies*, 314.

3. Augustine's last theological opponent, Julian of Eclanum, protested that "nothing in Scripture suggests that God is unjust" (*c. Iul.* 5.1.3).

Nevertheless, the doctrine of original sin does not obviate the incompatibility of a God who "first loved us" (1 John 4:19), yet abandoned most of the human race to the company of the damned.[4]

Until recently I have been content to juggle St. Augustine's ostensibly dissonant teachings, finding reassurance and delight in his many ardent descriptions of God's love, and leaving to God, as he repeatedly counseled, that *other* aspect of God.[5] In short, I understood Augustine selectively. This chapter describes my effort to understand the "whole Augustine," that is, how Augustine could love the God in whom he believed.

Readers usually assume that to understand an author is to "make sense" of his ideas and arguments, that is, to identify the internal consistency of his thought. Certainly, Augustine indefatigably endeavored to clarify his thinking in sermons, treatises, and letters.[6] However, if one seeks to understand an author as rich and complex as St. Augustine, the task is compounded; one must *aspire* to reconstruct the *perspective* from which the author spoke, or at least to acknowledge and identify the salient factors that must be considered. Moreover, a description of the values that shaped Augustine's perspective must be documented rather than intuited, an endeavor enabled by the fact that Augustine's "silent thoughts" (assumptions)[7] are not so silent; he repeated them frequently. In this article I focus on two themes to which he returned again and again in preaching and writing, namely, 1) the role of feeling in thinking and acting, and 2) his insistence on humility as the essential posture of a Christian.

---

4. Couenhoven, "St. Augustine's Doctrine,"359–96; also Burns, "Human Agency," 45–71; see also Ticciati, *New Apophaticism*.

5. *Perseu.* 11.25: "We live ... more securely if we give the whole to God, and do not entrust ourselves partly to him and partly to ourselves"; trans. Mourant and Collinge, *Four Anti-Pelagian Writings*, 281.

6. Augustine's *Ep.* 163 to Sapida, a consecrated virgin who mourned her brother, is an example of a classical consolation genre adopted and adapted to Christian belief in immortality.

7. A phrase used frequently by Michel Foucault to indicate an unexamined assumption that "silently" influences thinking.

Beautiful Bodies

I begin by specifying my working assumptions. First, I assume that St. Augustine's passionate and meticulous mind did not permit him to hold incompatible ideas. I seek, then, to understand why ideas that seem to me to be in opposition, may not have seemed so to Augustine. Indeed, apparent contradictions may reveal nothing more than vast differences between his assumptions and mine (held more or less in common with contemporaries in North American universities). For example, strongly influenced by Descartes's vastly influential segregation of mental from physical activity,[8] a distinction pictured in the West as the mythical centaur with a human head and a beast's body,[9] we (twenty-first-century academics) are likely to read our assumptions back into Augustine, who lived more than a thousand years before Descartes. In brief, Augustine did not consider the separation of feeling and thinking possible, let alone desirable.[10]

Therefore, to comprehend St. Augustine's teaching, it is requisite—but insufficient—to reconstruct his reasoning; readers must also notice and take into account the *feeling* that played an important role in his thinking. Readers must notice what we have not been trained to notice—or worse, have been trained *not* to notice—as we study Augustine's ideas. Augustine did not ignore his *feeling* in order to think; rather, he considered feeling, both physical and emotional, an essential ingredient of thinking. His feeling need not be at the mercy of readers' projections, for he frequently described the central importance of feeling in his life.

---

8. Descartes, *Meditations* VI: "I cannot see anything else that belongs necessarily to my nature or essence except that I am a thinking thing . . . a substance whose whole nature or essence is to think . . . [and] I have a distinct idea of the body as a thing that is extended and does not think."

9. For a contemporary neuroscientist on the impossibility of separating thought from feeling, see Antonio Damasio, *Feeling and Knowing*, 28.

10. One of Augustine's words for "reason" is *animus*; it is usually translated as "mind." However, *Cassell's Latin Dictionary* lists the first meaning of *animus* "the spiritual or rational principle of life, the *seat of feeling*, the heart."

How St. Augustine Could Love the God in Whom He Believed

FEELING

The young Augustine (described in his *Confessions*), thought that he must make a rational choice between the pursuit of secular ambition or God's service. Both attracted him.[11] He thought of the decision as a choice between a quiet life of monastic discipline and a prestigious and well-remunerated public life as a married professor of rhetoric. He considered his choice to be between incompatible ways of life.

As a student and teacher of rhetoric, Augustine knew that "contradiction" relates to rationality. Statements may contradict one another; feelings do not. Conflicting feelings are more complex. His account of his struggle states repeatedly that he was fully *convinced* to choose God's service *before* the emotional crisis of his choice occurred: "my mind was made up; I no longer had any doubt. . . . I no longer desired to be more certain of you [God]; there was no longer any reason for me to doubt; now I could see the truth perfectly clearly."[12] What is usually referred to simply as "Augustine's conversion," describes, not an impasse of rational thought, but a crisis of feeling.[13]

Introducing this life-altering experience, Augustine asked God to resolve and energize, not his understanding, but rather, his feeling: "Come, Lord, act upon us, rouse us up and call us back! Fire us, clutch us, let your sweet fragrance grow upon us. Let us love, let us run! . . . Let my bones be penetrated with your love."[14] The divided will he described was not caused by contradictory ideas, nor was it even a choice between incompatible ways of life; it was an

---

11. *Conf.* 8.5; trans. Warner, *Confessions*, 168. Later Augustine clarified his understanding of will (*uoluntatem*) in *De trinitate* (*trin.*) 15.21.41; trans. McKenna, *St. Augustine*, 518: "will . . . experiences various emotions . . . according to whether the things it encounters either entice or repel us; love . . . is a stronger will."

12. *Conf.* 8.1; trans. Warner, *Confessions*, 160.

13. *Conf.* 7 describes Augustine's rational perplexities: the origin of evil and its resolution (7.12–13), the importance of humility (7.9–10, 15, 18–19); astrology (7.6, 8.1; 8.5).

14. *Conf.* 8.4; trans. Warner, *Confessions*, 166; also 8.1, 160.

Beautiful Bodies

intense deadlock of conflicting feelings, evident in convulsive tears and flailing limbs. The passage describes Augustine's discovery that *will does not obey reason*. Rather, will is a volatile conglomerate that *includes* reason, memory, and desire, together with the domineering force of habit (*uiolentia consuetudinis*). At the time of his conversion to celibacy, it was these clashing energies that produced the strong conflict he experienced. Augustine learned from experience that *feeling* is the arena in which God works.

> God does something in us, I do not know what, in a spiritual, non-material way; it is neither a sound to strike the ears, nor a color to be distinguished by the eyes, nor a smell to be picked up by the nostrils, nor a flavor to be judged by the palate, nor something hard or soft to be felt by touching; all the same, it is something *easy to feel* (*sentire*) and impossible to explain.[15]

Fast forward a decade or so: As Augustine chose and pursued a life dedicated to God's service, he found that his choice had not been between incompatible ways of life, after all, but among binaries. Binaries present as opposites, but they are not resolved by adopting one and renouncing the other; rather the advantages of each must be sought, and the dangers of each avoided. Although quiet for study and meditation persistently eluded him in his busy public life as bishop, judge in the episcopal court, preacher, and pastor, it is evident in everything he spoke or wrote that he *made time* for study and meditation. He was also—albeit without choosing it—heir to the considerable social prestige and religious authority of a Christian bishop.[16]

---

15. *Io. eu. tr.* 40.5; trans. Hill (somewhat altered), *Gospel of John 1–40*, 598–99. Translations of "sentire" as "to perceive": "to apprehend with the mind," reveal the translator's "silent," that is, unexamined assumption that God works through the mind, although the passage says something quite different; God's activity is "easy [*facile*] to feel," but "impossible [*impossibile*] to explain."

16. Harrison, *Art of Listening*, 50: "Christian bishops [in the fourth and fifth centuries], a good number of whom had been former rhetoricians, lawyers, or governors, became ... the new educated aristocracy ... the holders of tremendous prestige, status, and power."

How St. Augustine Could Love the God in Whom He Believed

St. Augustine's attentiveness to feeling did not end in his youth. His sermons, especially those of his last decade, candidly refer to his current physical and emotional feeling—to his affective response to the Scripture on which he was preaching, to his "fear and trembling" over the heavy responsibility of preaching, or to his pleasure when the exuberant acclamations of his congregation demonstrated that they understood and appreciated his point.

Augustine continued to learn throughout his life, both from Scripture and from his experience. He understood humility, a posture he repeatedly advocated in sermons, letters, and treatises, to be essential to learning. We need read no further than his endlessly fascinating *Confessions* to recognize how diligently, as a relatively new Christian, he explored his experience in order to identify God's interior leading. As he matured, however, Augustine transitioned from self-identity based on individual experience, to communal self-identity as a member of the body of Christ.[17] The old Augustine was replete with a lifetime of experience, learning, and loving.

HUMILITY

The proud young Augustine's secular training did not encourage him to value humility: "Humility was not a subject which those [Platonist] books would ever have taught me."[18] Augustine's image of its opposite, pride, is graphic: As a young teacher who "sought the reputation of a wise man," he wrote, "it was as though my cheeks had swollen up so that I could not see out of my eyes."[19] Literally, pride blinds, preventing learning: "He who has convinced himself that he already knows, cannot learn."[20]

---

17. Grove, *Augustine on Memory*, 140, 182. Based on Augustine's sermons on the Psalms (Augustine's longest work, both in time and in length), Grove describes Augustine's reconstructed self-identity "beyond the self and within the whole body of Christ." See also Marion, *In the Self's Place*.

18. *Conf.* 7.19; trans. Warner, *Confessions*, 156.

19. *Conf.* 7.7; trans. Warner, *Confessions*, 146.

20. *Util. cred.* 11.25; trans. Meagher, *Advantage of Believing*, 425.

Beautiful Bodies

Augustine discovered humility in the human Jesus, whose humility was demonstrated by his willingness to accept a human body.[21] Readers can picture Augustine trembling as he permitted himself briefly to imagine a future in which he had not understood "divinity in the weakness that it had put on [by] wearing our coat of skin, [thus] healing the swelling of pride and fostering love." He wrote: "If I had not sought the way to you in Christ Jesus our Savior, what would have been finished would have been my soul."[22]

Throughout his teaching and writing, Augustine frequently contrasted the opposite and opposing feelings, pride and humility. Defining pride as "joy in oneself," he considered it the gravest of sins.[23] Commenting on 1 Cor 1:31: "He who takes pride should take pride in the Lord," Augustine, perhaps uncomfortable with the suggestion that pride *could* be praiseworthy, said that taking pride in the Lord was *actually* humility, the opposite of "joy in oneself." Moreover, in this life, in which no one is without sin, pride always lurks. It is the most insidious of sins because it can infiltrate and closely resemble charity. Pride can motivate feeding the hungry and clothing the naked; in fact, there is no good work which cannot be motivated by pride. "In the works themselves we can see no difference."[24] Augustine went so far as to say that "the humble sinner is better than the proud just man."[25]

Nor is humility a temporary "entrance level" expedient; according to Augustine, it is, rather, the quintessential lifelong character of a Christian:

> The way is firstly humility, second humility, third humility, and however often you should ask me I would say the same, not because there are not other precepts to be explained, but if humility does not precede and accompany and follow every good work we do, and if it is not

---

21. *Conf.* 7.18–19; trans. Warner, *Confessions*, 155.

22. *Conf.* 7.20; trans. Warner, *Confessions*, 157.

23. *En. ps.* 31, expos. 2: "You are impious and proud if you rejoice in yourselves . . . joy, rather, in God"; trans. Boulding, *Expositions of the Psalms*, 334.

24. *Ep. Io. tr.* 8.9; trans. Burnaby, *Ten Homilies*, 322.

25. *S.* 170.7; trans. Hill, *Sermons* III/5, 242.

set before us to look upon, and beside us to lean upon, and behind us to fence us in, pride will wrest from our hand any good deed we do while we are in the very act of taking pleasure in it.[26]

ST. AUGUSTINE PREACHING[27]

Interest in Augustine's sermons has recently been stimulated by Carol Harrison's *The Art of Listening in the Early Church*, and Kevin Grove's *Augustine on Memory*. In these and other works,[28] readers become acquainted with Augustine as pastor, friend, and fellow Christian, rather than the senescent preacher sometimes caricatured in commentaries.[29] Grove has demonstrated that Augustine's sermons give access to his "first order theology"—that is, in sermons

---

26. *Ep.* 118.3; trans. Parsons, *St. Augustine*, 282. See also *uirg.* 33; trans. Walsh, *Augustine*, 111. Augustine said that Jesus was crucified in order to "teach the lesson of humility." Homily 2.4; trans. Hill, *Sermons* III/1, 59.

27. Pierre-Patrick Verbraken, OSB, in his foreword to Hill, *Sermons* III/1, 11, notes that 548 of St. Augustine's sermons (complete or fragmentary), have been identified, and yet "we have only one-tenth or even one-fourteenth of all Augustine's sermons."

28. For example, Sanlon, *Augustine's Theology*.

29. Lamentably, old age is caricatured in modern society. For example, Edmund Hill, OP, translator of Augustine's sermons for NCP remarks that a sermon of Augustine's can be dated to his last years by "what I sense as the grandfatherly tone and occasional incoherency or falterings in the argument" (Hill, *Sermons* III/1, 371). Or: a sermon's "rather rambling quality, and occasional inconsequential train of thought, suggest an old man preaching" (Hill, *Sermons* III/2, 35n1). Or: a sermon "strikes me as coming from an older Augustine: I don't think he would have committed the rather glaring insequentiality of his final statement in his prime" (Hill, *Sermons* III/2, 172n1). Or: Hill suggests a late date for a sermon because "the grammar is at times rather slovenly and shows a looseness of style that will hardly permit us to assign [it] to Augustine's four years as a priest" (Hill, *Sermons* III/2, 179). Hill's more generous view of Augustine's last sermons, namely that Augustine "mellowed with age," is also a caricature (Hill, *Sermons* III/2, 206n1). I suggest that these sermons could be dated within Augustine's old age, rather, by his conversational tone, compassion for his hearers, and confident solidarity with his congregation within the body of Christ.

Beautiful Bodies

Augustine introduced and began to work out the implications of ideas that can be recognized later in his theological treatises.[30]

Then as now, theological language is unfamiliar to most people. Lacking familiarizing metaphors, it is difficult to hear "in the heart." Preaching, Augustine endeavored to bring abstract-sounding words to concreteness and immediacy, translating theological language as richly as possible with metaphors, similes, and analogies.[31] Nevertheless, skilled as he was in the arts of communication, St. Augustine was discouraged with spoken language's inability to communicate inner experience.[32]

In sermons at the Basilica Pacis in Hippo, Augustine often referred to his own experience, inviting listeners to experience with him. This was not merely an effective rhetorical strategy; it also reminded hearers of the spiritual consanguinity of members of the body of Christ. In the prayer Jesus gave his followers, he invited them to assume a family relationship with God: "our Father." Augustine declined to position himself as an authority within the body of Christ. The following quotations are not incidental asides; they are part of the message Augustine wanted to communicate to his congregation.

> Given my limitations I grasp what I set before you; when the door is opened,
>   I am nourished together with you;
> When it is shut, I knock together with you.[33]
>
> And so, my dearest friends, let me tell you what I think about the subject,

---

30. Grove, *Augustine on Memory*, 8.

31. Freud observed that the function of metaphors is to make hearers comfortable: "Analogies prove nothing; that is quite true, but they can make one feel more at home." See Strachey, *Sigmund Freud*, 837.

32. Augustine remarked in *De catechizandis rudibus* 46, 122 (*cat. rud.*); trans. Canning, *Instructing Beginners*: "I am nearly always dissatisfied with the address I give. For the address I am so eager to offer is the superior one which I enjoy again and again in my inner being. . . . And when I find that my actual address fails . . . to express what I have before my mind, I am sad that my tongue has not been able to keep up with my intellect."

33. *Io. eu. tr.* 18.1; trans. Hill, *Gospel of John 1–40*, 321.

> without prejudice to anything better you may have perceived. This is my opinion, and it is for you to see whether what I think is true,
> or comes close to the truth.[34]
>
> What am I? I'm a man; I'm the same as you; I am burdened with flesh;
> I am weak. The whole human life is short.
> The only pleasure I have in this life is your good life.[35]

Foregrounding his desire, his longing, his pleasure, St. Augustine spoke not only of his beliefs, but also—and often—of his feeling. He invoked the shared vulnerability and brevity of human life, seeking listeners who, like himself, feel and love vividly: "love with me" (*amate mecum*).[36]

> Give me a lover, and that one feels [*sentit*] what I am saying. Give me one who desires, one who hungers, one who wanders in the exile and thirsts, one who sighs for the fountain of the eternal homeland. Give me such a one, and that one knows what I say. But if I speak to one whose heart is cold, that one knows nothing of what I am saying.[37]

A preacher's ability to create in his hearers the *feeling* he described—whether vulnerability or delight—is an essential component of persuasion. Harrison writes:

> To take delight in what one is saying, to be able to communicate that delight so that the hearer is drawn to participate in it and share it is, for Augustine, the spark which ignites the fuse of effective communication between speaker and hearer: the delight of the one kindles that of the other, engages the attention, motivates the will, and inspires action.[38]

---

34. *Io. eu. tr.* 16.3; trans. Hill, *Gospel of John 1–40*, 298.
35. *S.* 17.6–7; trans. Hill, *Sermons* III/1, 370–71.
36. *Io. eu. tr.* 40.10; trans. Hill, *Gospel of John 1–40*, 603.
37. *Io. eu. tr.* 26.4; trans. Hill, *Gospel of John 1–40*.
38. Harrison, *Art of Listening*, 130.

Unlike the opposites pride and humility, each of which effectively cancels the other, St. Augustine frequently found binaries useful in preaching on the Christian life.[39] Binaries such as forgetting and remembering, weakness and strength, labor and rest, and solitude and communion, are not resolved by adopting one and renouncing the other, but by discerning the negative and positive effects of each. He explored the effects of fear and love in his sermons on the First Epistle of John (Eastertide 415 CE), summarizing the value of fear with a homely metaphor:

> When we sew a seam, the thread must be let in by the needle; the needle goes in first, but it must come out if the thread is to follow. So fear takes first hold upon the mind, but does not stay there, because the purpose of its entry was to let love in.[40]

Augustine's sermons address his listeners' feeling. As is clear in his analogy of the needle puncturing (fabric) so that the thread can enter, he regarded fear as an indispensable "needle," creating an opening for love. Augustine also had a great deal to say about the positive uses of chaste fear, and the negative uses of *amor* (*concupiscentia*).[41] Until late in his life, Augustine treated fear and love as binaries; however, as he approached death, discussed below, he no longer thought of fear and love in this way.

St. Augustine's last decade was engaged in uncompromising and voluble defense of the doctrines of predestination and perseverance. None of the recognized theological authorities was decisive in determining his position, though each played a role in forming his conviction. He denied that his obdurate stance resulted from reasoning, for "incomprehensible are his judgments and inscrutable are his ways" (quoting Rom 11:33). He considered Scripture authoritative and quoted it fluently, but his antagonists also employed a strong arsenal of scriptural support. Moreover, Augustine's appeal

---

39. Grove, *Augustine on Memory*, 159.
40. *Ep. Io. tr.* 9.4; trans. Burnaby, *Ten Homilies*, 332.
41. Augustine explained that "amor" is a neutral word; "dilectio" refers to spiritual love; "concupiscentia" designates desire for sex, power, or possessions; *ep. Io. tr.* 8.5; trans. Burnaby, *Ten Homilies*, 325.

to the church's practice of baptizing infants reversed the traditional relationship of theology and practice, citing practice as a basis for theology; Augustine claimed that infant baptism *assumes* and teaches that newborn infants are already contaminated by Adam's sin, and thus are in need of baptismal cleansing.[42] He denied that his teaching on the subject was new, and quoted several theological predecessors; none, however, decisively corroborated Augustine's full understanding. We must look elsewhere for his emphatic defense of the doctrine of predestination.

It is important to consider not only what a doctrine *says,* but also what it *does*—what it is likely to produce in the consciousness and actions of those who believe it. While predestination and perseverance overtly emphasize God's power, mercy, and grace, their *subjective* effect, the *feeling* generated, is humility—St. Augustine's *sine qua non* of the Christian life. Augustine has been called a rigorist in doctrine;[43] he is such, I suggest, because he understood the crucial importance of the doctrines of predestination and perseverance to Christian *life,* a life characterized by feeling and its ancillary, humility. In fact, as Julian noticed, St. Augustine did not urge his hearers and readers to "try harder."[44]

PREACHING PREDESTINATION

Augustine recognized that there was potentially a problematic dissonance between his consistent teaching that "both the

---

42. Augustine also cited church practice as support for his theology of prayer; because the church has always prayed that people might believe, and might persevere, "it has indeed always been believed that [these] were gifts of God"; *Perseu.* 23.65; trans. Mourant and Collinge, *Four Anti-Pelagian Writings,* 334. Also *nat. et grat.* 16.17; trans. Teske, *Answer to the Pelagians,* 232: "Why do we pray to receive it, if it is from man that it is to be had?"

43. Meer, *Augustine the Bishop,* 572.

44. Julian of Eclanum complained that Augustine's doctrine of original sin promotes immorality: "The crowds really love it when you blame defects of nature on the impurity of nature . . . the result is no one needs to try to change." *C. Iul. opus imperf.* 2.15; trans. Teske, *Answer,* 168.

beginning of faith and its end are gifts of God,"[45] and his strong interest in cultivating and encouraging his congregants' Christian life. In fact, interlocutors questioned whether—and if so, how—these doctrines could be preached without fatally subverting "the usefulness of preaching."[46] Nevertheless, in spite of the danger of mortally discouraging those who fear themselves among the *massa damnata*, and tempting those who consider themselves among the elect to slacken their Christian practice, Augustine said: "It is necessary to preach this predestination of God's favors; it must be preached, *so that he who has ears to hear may glory, not in himself, but in the Lord.*"[47]

Augustine conceded that the doctrine of predestination must be preached carefully. He cited precedent and multiple scriptural passages on the role and importance of preaching before describing his own approach to preaching predestination. "In the circumstances of earthly life," he said, he preached *as if* each hearer had "ears to hear";[48] those who have ears to hear will hear *in the heart*; those who do not will simply not hear. "Bear in mind," he said, "that we are not speaking to people in general, but to the Church of Christ."[49] He wrote:

> On predestination the set determination of the will of God is such that some of you having received the will to obey, have passed from unbelief to faith. What need

---

45. *Perseu.* 21.54.

46. Prosper of Aquitane, a layperson (*Ep.* 225), and Hilary, bishop of Arles (*Ep.* 226), wrote to Augustine (probably in 429 CE), citing "the opinion of some," that "exhorting anyone is useless if it is said that nothing is left in man which could be aroused by correction." Trans. Parsons, *St. Augustine*, 134.

47. *Perseu.* 20.51 (emphasis added). Despite Augustine's insistence that predestination must be preached, Cardinal Michele Pellegrino observed that "some especially knotty questions rarely appear in Augustine's sermons; for example, the problems connected with divine foreknowledge and predestination." "General Introduction," in Hill, *Sermons* III/1, 57.

48. *Io. eu. tr.* 18.10; trans. Hill, *Gospel of John*, 330–331: "Do you not have ears in the heart? ... Do you not have eyes in the heart? ... Your heart both sees and hears. ... In your heart you hear with what you see with."

49. *Perseu.* 22.60; trans. Mourant and Collinge, *Four Anti-Pelagian Writings*, 329.

is there to say "some of you?" For if we are speaking to the Church of God, if we are speaking to believers, why do we say that *some* of them have come to faith, and thus seem to do ill to the others, since we can more aptly say, "On predestination, the set determination of the will of God is such that, having *received* the will to obey, you have passed from unbelief to faith and, having *received* perseverance, you remain in faith."[50]

The key words in the quotation above are the repeated phrase, "having received." These words underline Augustine's insistence that neither predestination nor perseverance result from an individual's initiative or effort, though the individual's assent and cooperation is necessary. Nevertheless, "our very heart and our thoughts are not in our own power,"[51] but are also the gift of grace. Augustine frequently repeated "yet" (*tamen*) in his discussion of the necessity of preaching predestination: those who are predestinated but have not *yet* been called may be moved to hear "in the heart." Still, in the "circumstances of earthly life," he found this doctrine difficult to communicate to people unaccustomed to hearing theological concepts "in the heart."

One of Augustine's most difficult and puzzling themes was the interaction of grace and human response; he pointedly declined to specify the role of each.[52] Supported by quotations from Ambrose and Cyprian ("nothing is our own"),[53] he insisted that both God's grace and a person's grateful response are necessary: "we do it . . .

---

50. *Perseu.* 22.58.

51. *Perseu.* 19.50. Augustine cited his own youth as evidence that "God converts to himself men's wills, both those turned away from him and those turned against him." In his youth, Augustine himself not only "turned away," but also "turned against" God, "laying waste with most miserable and raging loquacity"; *Perseu.* 20.53; trans. Mourant and Collinge, *Four Anti-Pelagian Writings*, 321.

52. *Retr.* 1.23.2: "Both believing and willing are his because he readies the will, and both are ours because nothing is done unless we will it."

53. Cyprian, *Ad quirinum* 3.4; Ambrose, *De fuga saeculi* 1.1. Also *Perseu.* 19.48 and *De correption et gratia* 7.12: "the unpredestinated forsake and are forsaken"; trans. Murray, *Admonition*.

Beautiful Bodies

but God makes us do it."[54] Because God works *intus*, in the heart, Augustine found it both impossible and unhelpful to sort out who does what, when. Indeed, "we live more securely if we give up the whole to God, and do not entrust ourselves partly to him and partly to ourselves."[55] Ultimately, Augustine preferred to err in the direction of placing predestination in God's power.[56] Again, his primary purpose for preaching predestination was "so that he who has ears to hear may glory, *not in himself, but in the Lord*."

St. Augustine preached *as if* each member of his congregation was among the elect, but he also suggested some "tells." He quoted 1 Cor 9:24: "So run that you may obtain [the prize], and thus, by your very running you may know yourselves to be foreknown to be those who should run legitimately [*legitime*]." In other words, the predestined can find clues to their predestination to election in their own *apparently* voluntary cooperation. He also suggested that the unpredestined participate in their own fate; they simultaneously "forsake and are forsaken."[57]

Another evidence of the operation of grace in the life of a Christian is delight in the good: "Delight orders the soul; where the soul's delight is, there is its treasure."[58] However, as Peter Brown pointed out, this apparently soothing aphorism is also frightening, since no one can choose what gives them delight—Augustine's point exactly. Brown writes:

> It is just this vital capacity to engage one's feelings on a course of action, to take delight in it that escapes our powers of self-determination: The processes that prepare [a person's] heart to take delight in God are not only hidden but actually unconscious and beyond [our] control.[59]

---

54. *Praed.* 11.22; also 3.7.
55. *Perseu.* 11.25; quoted above (n. 5).
56. Burns, "Human Agency," 65.
57. *Corrept.* 13.42: "deserunt et deseruntur."
58. *Mus.* 6.11.29; trans. Talliaferro, *On Music*, 355.
59. Brown, *Augustine*, 155.

Finally, Augustine's sermons advocate "hope in the Lord": "far be it from you to despair of yourselves, since you are commanded to place your hope in him and not in yourselves."[60] He found it astonishing that some would rather trust themselves than God.[61] To the all-too-human longing to gain some small sense of control of one's life, St. Augustine counseled the humility requisite to "leave it to God." Augustine's most often quoted Scripture verse says it all, both the impossibility of present knowledge, and the hope of future fulfillment: "Uidemus *nunc* per speculum in aenigmate; *tunc* autem facie ad faciem" (1 Cor 13:12). Hope is prepared by long commitment to "walking along the road" by faith:

> One is not only instructed so as to see you . . . but also so as to grow strong enough to hold you, and one who cannot see you for the distance, may yet walk along the road by which he will arrive and see you and hold you.[62]

Preaching predestination, St. Augustine seems to have realized the perfect coalescence of two vocabularies, theological language and that of his own experience. How else to comprehend the *in-side* of his experience, in which he was "dragged [*raperes*] by the force of [his] own desires"—that is, by the very desires that he thought were his *own most intimate*, rebellious, defiant, and lustful cravings? I conjecture that Augustine could explain to himself the mystery of his experience in no other way than by the mind-boggling doctrine of predestination.

CONCLUSION

In conclusion, I collect from St. Augustine's writings his understanding of God-is-love in relation to his intransigent adherence to the doctrines of predestination and perseverance. I seek to

---

60. *Perseu* 22.62; trans. Mourant and Collinge, *Four Anti-Pelagian Writings*, 330.

61. *Praed. sanct.* 11.21; trans. Mourant and Collinge, *Four Anti-Pelagian Writings*, 243: "I am amazed that men would rather trust in their own weakness than in the strength of God's promise."

62. *Conf.* 7.21; my translation.

Beautiful Bodies

understand him as a bishop, pastor, and preacher, committed to the doctrines and practices of the church, to Scripture, to his experience, and also to the support and encouragement of his hearers.

First: Of primary and essential importance is St. Augustine's description of God as "life itself" (*uitam ipsam*): "Only they can think of God without absurdity who think of him as life itself."[63] By "life itself," he explained, he did not refer to "Life"—an abstraction—but rather to an intimate living reality, namely, "God is *the life of your life*" (*tibi uae uits est*).[64] Although predestination is neither (strictly speaking) experiential, nor does it yield to rational explanation, predestination is a concrete reality *abstracted* as a theological verity; in experience, in *feeling*, it is simply "what there is," "life itself, the life of [my] life."[65]

Second: Describing visionary experiences in *conf.* 7.17 and 9.10. Augustine did not say that he *saw* God in any of the ways he carefully delineated: corporeal, intellectual, or spiritual.[66] Nor did he say that God was revealed to him through one of God's appellations (Light, Truth, Wisdom, Love, etc.). He said that what he saw/touched was simply "what there is" (*id quod est*).

Third: If God is "uitam ipsam," to be recognized *within* the scatter of one's own experience, fear is a likely human response; Augustine's God, *accessible as one's own life,* is fundamentally unpredictable and "inscrutable." In the face of this reality, humans are both incorrigibly ignorant and terminally vulnerable. Augustine said in a sermon: "Aren't we more fragile than if we were made of

---

63. *Doct. chr.* 1.8; trans. Robertson, *On Christian Doctrine*, 12. Augustine wrote book 1 of *doct. chr.* c. 396 CE; when he completed the work thirty years later (c. 426), he did not alter or nuance this statement.

64. *Conf.* 10.6 (emphasis added): "God is for you too the life of your life, the very living life"; trans. Warner, *Confessions*, 59, 316; also 3.6, trans. Warner, *Confessions*.

65. "To abstract" is to extract an intellectual idea from a concrete reality. This is precisely St. Augustine's understanding of predestination. In other words, the phrase "life itself" is distilled (abstracted) from the intimate reality, "uae uits."

66. *De geneni ad litteram* 12.6.15; cited by Teske, "St. Augustine and the Vision of God," 293.

glass?"[67] The old Augustine knew from his own experience that humans *really* don't have much time, and within that short time, we do not control the gifts and the griefs—the occasions for potential learning—that come to us.

The sermons of Augustine's last fifteen years convey a strong sense of communal identity and empathy with his congregation. Perhaps this change of tone reflected his strengthened doctrine of original sin. To pause and reflect on this condition, he said, brings a suffocating sense of helplessness. We are stranded in circumstances we neither chose nor merited; we are weak (*uitium*), unshielded from the dark undertow of human life. To *feel* this vulnerability, not only in one's own life, but in all humanity, must arouse fear.

It is within this terrifying scenario that the role of the church, established and authorized by Jesus's miracles, can be understood. In the face of "id quod est"—*what there is*—the church offers a path, a mapped migration route from fear to love, in *communal identity* with a multitude of others, both those presently alive and those who have gone ahead, as body of Christ, together with Christ, the Head.

In one of his last sermons (429–30 CE), St. Augustine described his self-identity. He no longer understood himself as the sum of the personal experiences he had traced so carefully in his *Confessions*, but as a member of the body of Christ:

> What, after all, do I want? What do I desire? What am I longing for? Why am I speaking? Why am I sitting here? What do I live for, if not with this intention that we should *all live together with Christ*? That is my desire, that is my honor, that is my most treasured possession, that is my joy, my pride and glory.... I don't want to be saved without you.[68]

Individual self-identity produces fear, the instinct to protect and defend the frail self, an activity presuming self-sufficiency—in a word, pride.[69] Communal identity in the body of Christ relaxes

---

67. S. 17.6; trans. Hill, *Sermons* III/1, 371.

68. S. 17.2; trans. Hill, *Sermons* III/1, 367.

69. Grove characterized this position as being "stuck in the self," *Augustine on Memory*, 142–43.

the self's anxious self-preoccupation, its obsessive me-me-me, creating space for God's love to circulate freely. Communal identity does not erase individuality, rather its isolation is overcome. In the life and practices of the church—liturgy, ritual, hearing, seeing, eating, and drinking together—fear, the ineluctable affect of personal identity, is overwhelmed by love.

> When the hearts of the faithful . . . are cemented together with the bond of charity, it constitutes the beauty of God's house. . . . Anyone who loves the beauty of God's house loves the Church, not for the craftsmanship of its walls and roof, not for its shining marble and gilded ceilings, but for its faithful and holy members, who love God with all their heart and all their soul, and all their mind, and their neighbor as themselves.[70]

The urgent question St. Augustine addressed in preaching was how humans can live most richly *now* with "what there is" (*id quod est*). His answer, in brief, was "by loving, you see, we live from within."[71] His sermons on the First Epistle of John rave about the pleasure of God's love in the body of Christ: "Does it follow that he who loves his brother loves God also? Of necessity he must love God; of necessity he must love love itself. . . . In loving love he is loving God . . . for God is love."[72] "You cannot have a fuller commendation of love than the naming of it with God's name."[73] In these sermons, Augustine addressed a question he was frequently asked: Is it possible to see God in this life? Significantly, he did not urge members of his congregation to pursue a vision of God.[74] Rather, "in the circumstances of earthly life," he recommended, "if you would see God, God is love."[75]

---

70. *S.* 15.1; trans. Hill, *Sermons* III/1, 323.
71. *Io. eu. tr.* 2.11; trans. Hill, *Gospel of John 1–40*, 63; also 25.15.
72. *Ep. Io. tr.* 9.10; trans. Burnaby, *Ten Homilies*, 336.
73. *Ep. Io. tr.* 8.14; trans. Burnaby, *Ten Homilies*, 327.
74. *Ep.* 147, to Paulina (c. 413), "Vision of God," trans. Parsons, *St. Augustine*, 223.
75. *Ep. Io. tr.* 7.4; trans. Burnaby, *Ten Homilies*, 314.

How St. Augustine Could Love the God in Whom He Believed

Death, the final release of the individual self, gathers the Christian into the "whole Christ."[76] Christians can approach death as the ultimate humble abnegation of effort toward one's own salvation; "leave it to God," as Augustine counseled.[77] "There is good hope for that man whom the last day of his life shall find progressing so that whatever was wanting to his progress may be added to him, and that he should be judged rather to need perfecting than punishment."[78] Augustine anticipated that his lifelong commitment to learning would remain with him through death, as it had in life.

The God who predestines, revealed in Scripture, defended by apostolic authority, and declared in the church by doctrine and practice, has not disappeared. Neither has the *intellectual* incompatibility between the doctrines of predestination and the God who *is* love been resolved. But the *feeling* of the Christian who has "walked along the road"[79] in the companionship of Christ's body is absorbed into God-is-love. St. Augustine's last sermons spoke poignantly, movingly, of his own expectation: "Fear should grow less," he said, "the closer we approach to our home country [and] those who are arriving will have none at all.... What has put fear out the door... is the love of God, whom you are loving with your whole heart and with your whole soul and with your whole mind."[80] Arriving home, immersed in God's love, doctrines (such as predestination and perseverance) are effortlessly "left to God." Unlike fear, humility goes all the way; as surrounding love increases, humility does not evaporate, but is absorbed into love, for "it is superfluous to worry that humility will be lacking when there is radiant love."[81]

---

76. Grove, *Augustine on Memory*, 110: "Augustine the preacher does not conform to scholarly presentations of the elderly bishop and thinker whose optimism about humanity darkens as he ages.... Augustine's work from this period is characterized by enjoyment in Christ."

77. *Perseu.* 6.12.

78. *Perseu.* 21.55; my translation.

79. *Conf.* 7.21; trans. Warner, *Confessions*, 158.

80. *S.* 348.2; trans. Hill, *Sermons* III/10, 92, 94.

81. *Uirg.* 54; trans. Walsh, *Augustine*, 40, slightly altered.

Chapter Four

St. Augustine's Tears
Recollecting and Reconsidering a Life

IN AUGUSTINE'S SOCIETY, MEN'S tears were not considered a sign of weakness, but an expression of strong feeling. Tears might be occasional, prompted by incidents such as those Augustine described in the first books of his *Confessions*. Or they might accompany a crisis, such as his conversion to celibacy. Possidius, Augustine's contemporary biographer, reported that on his deathbed Augustine wept copiously and continuously. This chapter seeks to understand those tears, finding, primarily but not exclusively in Augustine's later writings, descriptions of his practice of meditation, suggesting that a profound and complex range of emotions from fear and repentance to gratitude, love, rest in beauty, peace, and delight in praise richly informed Augustine's last tears.[1]

INTRODUCTION

Several years before his death, Augustine undertook to review his published works. In his *Retractationes (retr.)*, Augustine

---

1. The St. Augustine Lecture, 2019 at Villanova University was a version of this chapter.

reconsidered many of his publications, correcting infelicitous or, he feared, misleading language. He read his writings in roughly chronological order, intending to include in his survey not only treatises but also his sermons and letters. However, distracted by heated correspondence with Julian of Eclanum, he did not complete his project. Having reviewed ninety-three of his publications, he abandoned the project in 427 CE, three years before his death.

Several years ago I undertook a similar project. I read over fifty years of my publications, commenting critically on omissions, mistakes, and inadequate knowledge.[2] I recommend this exercise highly to retired scholars. There are substantial benefits to reviewing one's publications. Very occasionally, one is pleasantly surprised by one's perspicacity. More often, one is dismayed and humbled by its lack. Humility may not immediately appear to be a great benefit, but Augustine valued humility highly, going so far as to say, "The way is firstly humility, secondly humility, and thirdly humility."[3] Moreover, a review quilts one's work into a body, a *corpus*, revealing the values that directed one's attention, in short, what one *stood for* as a scholar. Reflection on one's *corpus* also inspires gratitude for the remarkable consanguinity of life and thought and for the immense privilege of scholarship.

The Old Augustine

The old Augustine has a bad press. Even loyal readers have found it difficult to appreciate his last embattled writings.[4] His doctrine of predestination, his identification of the transmission of original sin as occurring at the moment of conception, and his repetitive and pugnacious tone have made for difficult reading. John Burnaby,

---

2. Miles, *Recollections*, 2018.

3. *Ep.* 118.8.22.

4. Journalists often consider St. Augustine the enemy. For example, Greenblatt, "Invention of Sex," captioned "Spoiling the Fun." But see John Cavadini's argument that Augustine was the "true radical" against Julian's "sentimentalization of fallen human freedom." "Reconsidering Augustine," 189.

Beautiful Bodies

who has been called "one of Augustine's most perceptive admirers,"[5] wrote, "Nearly all that Augustine wrote after his seventieth year is the work of a man whose energy has burnt itself out, whose love has grown cold."[6] Peter Brown's 1967 *Augustine of Hippo*, characterized Augustine's conflict with Julian as "an unintelligent slogging match." However, Brown corrected his earlier judgment in the 2000 edition of the biography. Influenced by new evidence discovered by Johannes Divjak, Brown found rather that Augustine's last letters demonstrate "an inspired fussiness, [and a] heroic lack of measure when it came to the care of endangered souls."[7]

I will suggest, however, that in addition to doctrinal controversy, the old Augustine was engaged in tasks precisely appropriate to his stage of life.[8] An endemic ageism in scholarship neglects to notice that (even) the lives of saints and scholars have a shape; the tasks of later years consist less in groundbreaking new ideas than in collecting one's memories and in criticizing and clarifying one's ideas.[9] The perspective of many years can afford insight unattainable in earlier years. This vantage point does not appear automatically, but as the result of eager and thoughtful learning throughout life; Augustine simply called this responsiveness to learning "humility."

As Augustine lay dying, Vandals laid siege to Hippo. Augustine saw the destruction of his life's work.[10] One of Augustine's last letters contained advice to priests and bishops who consulted him concerning whether they were permitted to flee their ecclesiastical stations at the approach of the Vandals. A pastor to the end, Augustine's letter tirelessly (or, some readers may think, tiresomely) considered the Scriptures and precedents that seem to permit

5. Bonner, "Augustine and Mysticism," 139.
6. Burnaby, *Amor Dei*, 231; also O'Donnell: "the crabbed turmoil of Augustine's later years," in *Augustine*, 79.
7. Brown, *Augustine*, 466.
8. O'Donnell, "Next Life," 222: "Our biographical style . . . knows best . . . the narrative of youth and maturation. It does not know how to describe maturity and age, but struggles as best it can to impose its stereotypes."
9. Carruthers, *Craft*, 5: "People do not 'have' ideas, they 'make' them."
10. Possidius, *Uita*, 28; trans. Weiskotten, *Porphyry*, 4.

St. Augustine's Tears

flight, concluding that clergy may flee only if "there are no longer any persons to whom it is necessary to minister."[11] The siege of Hippo lasted fourteen months; Augustine died in the third month of the siege.[12]

Possidius, Bishop of Calama, who lived in Augustine's household for almost forty years in "intimate and delightful friendship,"[13] described Augustine's last days:

> In private conversations, Augustine told us that even praiseworthy Christians and bishops ... should not leave this life without having performed fitting and appropriate penance. And this he himself did in his last illness. ... For he commanded that the shortest penitential Psalms of David should be copied for him;[14] as he lay in bed looking at these sheets hanging on the wall, he wept copiously and constantly [*ubertime et iugiter*]. ... About ten days before he departed from the body he asked that no one should come in to him except when doctors came to examine him or when food was brought to him. This was observed and done, and he had all that time free for prayer.[15]

Why did Augustine request privacy in his last few days? Is this the same Augustine who, in mid-life so insouciantly revealed his youthful sins to readers? I suggest that Augustine the pastor, acutely sensitive to others' intellectual and spiritual needs, seems to have found it difficult or impossible to reflect on himself when distracted by others' questions and problems. He needed to be alone so that he could be "*by himself*,"[16] concentrated, undistracted by "the care of endangered souls."

---

11. Possidius, *Uita*, 30.1; trans. Weiskotten, *Possidius*, 119.

12. When Vandals ransacked Hippo, Augustine's library was left intact, the books carefully catalogued by Possidius.

13. Possidius, *Uita*, 31; trans. Weiskotten, *Possidius*, 59.

14. Psalms 6, 31, 129, 142.

15. Possidius, *Uita*, 31; trans. Weiskotten, *Possidius*, 56–57.

16. Arendt, *Life of the Mind*, 185: "When Socrates goes home he is not alone; he is *by himself*." Arendt describes solitude as "that human situation in which I *keep myself company*"; by contrast, "alone" connotes a lack of the company of others.

Nevertheless, according to Possidius's report, Augustine was not unaware of his contemporary influence. Like Plotinus sixty years earlier, he considered his own process of dying a "teachable moment."[17] In this chapter I reconsider Augustine's deathbed tears, assisted by his own descriptions of his practice of meditation, an exercise—to our ears—inadequately characterized by Possidius's shorthand description of Augustine's tears as penitential. Modern readers, accustomed to a flattened definition of "penance" as sorrow for sin, are not likely to grasp immediately the richer connotation of "penance" that Possidius, who lived in Augustine's household for forty years, may well have assumed and taken for granted. I will seek to demonstrate that Augustine's last tears were informed by a profound and complex range of emotions from fear and repentance to gratitude, love, rest in beauty, and delight in praise.

Augustine in *Confessions*

I begin, then, to gather the suggestions that will help us to understand Augustine's deathbed tears. We must start with his *Confessions*. In his *Retractationes*, Augustine said that his only work that he recalled with unmitigated pleasure was *Confessions*.

> The thirteen books of my confessions praise the just and good God for *both the bad and the good that I did,* and they draw a person's mind and emotions toward him. As for myself, that is how they affected me when they were being written, and that is how they affect me when they are being read. What others may think of them is up to them, but I know that they have pleased and do please many of the brothers a good deal.[18]

Why was *Confessions* pleasurable for Augustine? Surely the first nine books recount thoughts and actions of which the old bishop might reasonably be dismayed. And surely the brothers

---

17. Plotinus's last words, reported by his biographer, Porphyry, were: "Try to give back the god in you to the divine in the All." Trans. Armstrong, *Plotinus*, 7.

18. *Retr.* 2.6.94; trans. Ramsey, *Revisions*, 114; emphasis added.

who were pleased by Augustine's confessions did not find his youthful transgressions edifying. The answer, I think, is that Augustine enclosed "both the bad and the good that I did" (*malis et bonus meis*) *within* God's unerring leading. *This* was the narrative that gathered and wove together the colorful strands of his life.[19] God's omnipresent leading was the "cover story" within which Augustine collected his memories,[20] a narrative capacious enough to exclude none of his experience.[21] Perhaps the most remarkable sentence of this incredible book is Augustine's claim that (in retrospect) God's utterly trustworthy leading was operative even *within* his most rebellious behavior. None of his experience was wasted; he was "dragged by the force of [his] own desires" through the experiences by which he learned. Similarly, his unbearable youthful unhappiness prompted him to seek another life.

It is remarkable that Augustine did not simply sort his experience into two files, rejecting and ignoring what he identified as his "bad" and rejoicing in his "good" behavior. He was able to do this because of his idea of the appropriate attitude toward sin. After citing schoolboys' desires for "footballs, nuts, and pet sparrows" (which he did not hesitate to call "sin"), and the behavior of adults who lust after "gold, estates, and slaves," he expressed his astonishment—he marveled—reiterating for emphasis, that "no one is sorry for the children; no one is sorry for the older people; no one is sorry for both of them."[22] In Augustine's experience, the agenda of sin, extrapolated from the neonate's first gasp/grasp of breath, through infancy and childhood, to the objects of adult desire, is exhausting and painful. Empathy is the appropriate response. Understanding his life as intimately formed and informed by God's leading made it possible for Augustine to feel, for his own sin, the

19. *Conf.* 11.2; trans. Warner, *Confessions*, 194.

20. See O'Connell's discussion of *"fovisti caput,"* in *St. Augustine's Early Theory*, 65–86.

21. *Corrept.* 9.24; trans. Murray, *Admonition*, 274: "God makes all things work together for good—absolutely all things, even to the extent that if some of them swerve and stray from the path, he makes their very wanderings contribute to their good."

22. *Conf.* 1.9.

Beautiful Bodies

attitude he recommended for others' sin, namely, compassion. He characterized the relief of his conversion: "I relaxed a little from myself" and "I breathed a little in you [God]."[23]

Augustine frequently used characterizations for God, such as light, wisdom, truth, life, and beauty.[24] In *conf.* 10.27, beauty (*pulchritude tam antiqua et tam noua*)[25] was his preferred expression. God's beauty spoke loudly to him through his senses. When he asked the earth, the sea, the creeping things, the breezes, heaven, the sun, the moon, and the stars, "Tell me about my God," their answer, as beautiful creations of the great beauty, "was in their beauty."[26]

> What do I love when I love you? Not the beauty of the body nor the glory of time, not the brightness of light shining so friendly to the eye, not the sweet and various melodies of singing, not the fragrance of flowers and ointments and spices, not manna and honey, not limbs welcome to the embraces of the flesh: it is not these that I love when I love my God. And yet I do love a kind of light, melody, fragrance, food, and embrace when I love my God; for he is the light, the melody, the food, the fragrance, the embrace of my inner self—there where is a brilliance that space cannot contain, a sound that time cannot carry away, a perfume that no breeze disperses, a taste undiminished by eating, a clinging together that no satiety will sunder. This is what I love when I love my God.[27]

Describing his conversion to celibacy, Augustine employed the language of vivid sensory experience: "You called, you cried out, you shattered my deafness: you flashed, you shone, you scattered my blindness; you breathed perfume, and I drew in my

---

23. *Conf.* 7.14.20: "Cessaui de me paululum"; *Conf.* 13.14.15: "Respire in te paululum."
24. Hockenbery, "He, She, and It," 433–44.
25. *Conf.* 10.27.38.
26. *Conf.* 10.6.9.
27. *Conf.* 10.6.8; trans. Warner, *Confessions*, 214–15.

breath and I pant for you: I tasted, and I am hungry and thirsty; you touched me and I burned for your peace"[28]

Augustine's Youthful Tears

Male socialization in Augustine's society permitted men to weep.[29] Tears were understood to be an index, not of weakness, but of strong feeling. Historians of emotion contest the assumption that "emotions are [simply] a universal expression of human nature." They argue that societies develop "emotional styles, scripts, and patterns." Thus, the study of emotions must be based on "the historical vocabulary and underlying beliefs used in particular contexts."[30] Historian Piroska Nagy writes: "Most emotions lose part or all of their meaning, even their very reality, outside the cultural context that produces them."[31] In Western late antiquity the social significance of emotions is indicated by the fact that nuances of emotions are expressed by a rich vocabulary, including: "*preturbatio, inclinatio, motus animi, affectus, affectio,* and *passio*."[32]

In *Confessions* Augustine reported incidents of episodic or circumstantial tears. Most of the tears of his youth were of this kind: tears of frustration;[33] of physical pain;[34] of grief over the death of a beloved friend;[35] sentimental tears over a fictional character;[36]

28. *Conf.* 10.27.38; trans. Warner, *Confessions*, 235.
29. Nagy, "Power of Medieval Emotions," 16.
30. Nagy, "Power of Medieval Emotions," 19.
31. Nagy, "Power of Medieval Emotions," 25; Nagy comments: "Christian anthropology is built on the centrality of emotions, especially love and pain." Christine Mohrmann studied the dramatic change in meaning of the verb "patior" (to suffer) from a negative meaning in classical authors to a valued condition in Christian authors, "Saint Augustin écrivain," 52.
32. Nagy, "Power of Medieval Emotions," 24. Nuanced vocabulary attests the cultural significance of its objects, such as the nuanced vocabulary for snow in Alaska or rain in Seattle.
33. *Conf.* 1.6.7.
34. *Conf.* 9.4.9.
35. *Conf.* 4.4.7–7.12, and 9.12.29–13.37.
36. *Conf.* 3.2.2.

tears of jealousy;[37] grief over his mother's death;[38] and tears prompted by the sweetness of psalms sung in church.[39] Observers could readily identify the cause of most of Augustine's tears, but Possidius reported that Augustine also wept at his conscripted ordination; these were tears others found difficult to interpret.[40] But the tears Augustine described in *conf.* 8.12, tears prompted by an acute emotional and intellectual crisis of compunction and conversion, were his only youthful tears not prompted by external circumstance. At the moment of his conversion only an intimate friend who was experiencing a similar crisis understood Augustine's tears.[41]

Before we venture beyond *Confessions*, we must note for future reference that Augustine's confessions occurred *within* an act of praise. The first chapter of book one repeatedly insists:

> And humans want to praise you . . . humans who are only a small portion of what you have created, want to praise you. . . . You stimulate us to take pleasure in praising you because you have made us for yourself, and our hearts are restless until they rest in you.[42]

For Augustine, praise provided the framework—the frame—for confession, the appropriate response to God's leading through "both the bad and the good that I did."

When he wrote *Confessions*, Augustine expected and trusted that God's guidance would be the story of his life: "You [God] will carry us, yes, from our infancy until our grey hairs you will carry

---

37. *Conf.* 3.1.1.
38. *Conf.* 9.11.27—12.33.
39. *Conf.* 10.33.49-50.
40. Possidius, *Uita*, 4.
41. Carruthers, *Craft*, 176; Carruthers recognized patterns in Augustine's postures and gestures reported in *conf.* 8.12 that will later characterize medieval meditation, such as: "initial anguish expressed and maintained by continual weeping . . . mental imaging, repetition of Psalm *formulae*, and prone posture."
42. *Conf.* 1.1.1.

us."[43] Yet the Scripture verse he quoted more frequently than any other throughout his career recognized the inadequacy of present vision, 1 Cor 13:12: "*Uidemus nunc per speculum et in aenigmate; tunc autem facie ad faciem.*" At the time of writing, he was sharply aware that he walked "by faith and not by sight."[44] He had not yet experienced God's leading across his lifetime, and readers of *Confessions* have detected traces of anxiety among his confident affirmations.

Augustine's Second Thoughts

Augustine gathered the choices and actions of his life into a compendium of the whole; from that perspective he understood each moment as a necessary, albeit often painful, step within God's direction.[45] In order to support this narrative, he must repudiate two explanations of life's occurrences that had attracted him as a youth: first, the Academics' despair of finding truth; second, the notion that things happen by chance. The first chapters of the first book of *retr.* begins with Augustine's denunciation of hints of these ideas he detected in his early publications. His "clear and certain" conviction of God's leading rendered both unresolvable doubt and the whims of "fortune" unacceptable.[46]

Later, while he was working on *retr.*, Augustine noticed that an earlier work, *De doctrina christiana,* begun in 396 CE remained unfinished; he interrupted his present project to finish it.[47] Augustine realized—as part of his project of gathering his

---

43. *Conf.* 4.16.31.

44. 2 Cor 5:7; quoted at *conf.* 13.13.14.

45. O'Donnell points out historians' predilection for "a coherent narrative of a single life" rather than "fragmentation," in "Next Life," 221–22.

46. *Retr.* I.1-2. *Retr.* establishes Augustine's willingness to be rather harshly self-critical. Augustine called an earlier statement of his, "*inane et stultus*" ("inept and foolish"), *retr.* I.1.3; when confronted with an awkward question, he was willing to say, "I did not know then and I still do not know" (*retr.* 1.1.3).

47. Augustine abandoned *doctr. chr.* at 3.25.35, completing book three and all of book four c. 427 CE.

Beautiful Bodies

memories—that his education, training, and practice of rhetoric had far more influence on his life and work than he had recognized or acknowledged.[48] In *Confessions*, he had described reading Cicero's *Hortensius* when he was nineteen. It was not the book's style that moved him, he said, but its content, its "exhortation to philosophy.... I was on fire... that book inflamed me with the love of wisdom."[49] He reported that upon his conversion, he rejected the teaching and practice of rhetoric in favor of the study of Scripture, which subsequently laced his every mature communication.[50]

But clearly the older Augustine found his rhetorical training and the impact of Cicero on his life more influential than simply jump-starting him on his search for wisdom.[51] He recognized that his life story was incomplete, omitting as it did a description of the relationship of his training in rhetoric to his preaching, authorship, and—as I will discuss shortly—most importantly, to his relationship with his God. Old age prompted him to arc back over his middle years as bishop and author to gather even his preconversion experience, weaving it into his life narrative.

Augustine realized that in turning away from Cicero and his own youthful career he nevertheless brought his engagement with rhetoric with him.[52] He acknowledged that eloquence can assist the goals of teaching and preaching. Those who preach "dully, unevenly, and coldly," benefit hearers less, he said, than those who preach "acutely, ornately, and vehemently." He was careful to note that eloquence must be subordinated to effective communication: "the speaker should not consider the eloquence of his teaching but

---

48. *Conf.* I.18.29; trans. Warner, *Confessions*, 37.

49. *Conf.* 3.4.7.

50. Concerned to give rhetorical skills no more significance than they should have, Augustine demonstrated their thorough integration in his preaching by mentioning Cicero by name only in a footnote in *doctr. chr.* 4.12.27.

51. *Doct. chr.* 4.3.6; trans. Robertson, *On Christian Doctrine*, 120.

52. Augustine described his preaching in *cat. rud.* 3.5; trans. Carruthers, *Craft*, 65n18, 124–25: he dissected the Scripture of the day, offering it "one piece at a time as though to loosen it up or expand it, to offer it for inspection and wonder." Michael Cameron described Augustine's sermon style as "mastication of the text," in *"Totus Christus,"* 66.

only the clarity."[53] "There is no reason for speaking if what is said is not understood."[54]

Indeed, throughout his ministry, rhetorical skills, though subordinated to Scripture, informed his distinctive preaching style.[55] He seldom—if ever—used his own words if a scriptural word or phrase would strengthen his thought. He quoted Scripture both to reinforce and to attest the truth of his thought. Yet Augustine also realized that scriptural proficiency alone is insufficient; preachers and teachers must also "look into the heart of Scripture with the eye of their own hearts."[56] And, as discussed in the last section of this chapter, Augustine's rhetorical training deeply informed his ability to access the "eye" of his own heart.[57]

James O'Donnell has proposed the intriguing idea that St. Augustine's *retr.* should be considered volume two of his autobiography. *Conf.*, volume one, describes the young Augustine as passionate seeker, while *retr.*—volume two—establishes the mature Augustine as bishop, author, and defender of doctrine. But *retr.* exhibits none of the intellectual and emotional urgency of *Confessions*; Augustine did not weep as he dispassionately reconsidered his publications; he shed no tears over the mistakes, inadequate words and expressions, and *ad hominem* arguments that pepper his writings. We must look beyond *retr.* for reflections in which he was engaged both intellectually and emotionally.

---

53. *Doct. chr.* 4.9.23; trans. Robertson, *On Christian Doctrine*, 133.

54. *Doct. chr.* 4.10.24. St. Augustine would not have approved of Cyril of Alexandria's writing style, described by Robert Wilken as "an unhappy synergy of grandiloquence and affectation," in "Cyril of Alexandria's *Contra Iulianum*," 43.

55. Modern editors of fourth-century sermons use Augustine's vivid preaching style as a criterion to judge whether a sermon ascribed to Augustine is genuine; for example, Maurists decline attribution of *Sermons* 383, 384 to Augustine "on a point of style." See Hill, *Sermons* III/10, 382. Similarly, *S.* 351 was "probably not preached by Augustine" on grounds that "the sermon lacks the breath of life that marks Aug's preaching, even at its least inspired" (134).

56. *Doct. chr.* 4.5.7.

57. See Phillip Cary's discussion of Augustine's use of Cicero's theory of memory, in *Augustine's Invention*, 134–39.

Beautiful Bodies

Augustine's collection (*colligere*)[58] of his memories into the narrative of his life was, until his last days, an incomplete work. It was incomplete in *Confessions* because he did not, in early middle age, have the memories with which to furnish his life-story; it was incomplete in *retr.* because there he had focused on his published communications. I suggest that Augustine's deathbed tears might be considered a virtual volume three. "Volume three," regrettably but of necessity, while not Augustine's direct account, nevertheless is important to our understanding of his life and work.

Augustine has largely preoccupied scholars due, perhaps, to his formidable influence on doctrines and controversies.[59] The private Augustine has been given short shrift. Yet it is the private Augustine, occupied throughout his life with transforming his psychic "weight" from fear to love, who offers suggestions and an example that can be helpful to others similarly engaged.

In order to retrieve the private Augustine, we must consider his practice of meditation, as well-documented in his writings as were his youthful peccadilloes.[60] Meditation was central to Augustine's Christian practice; he devoted intellectual and emotional resources to cultivating his life *before God*.

First, some general observations on meditation in late antiquity and the Middle Ages; finally, St. Augustine's description of his own practice.

---

58. Hugh of St. Victor later defined *colligere*; to collect is "to reduce those things which are written or spoken about at greater length to a briefer and commodious summary. . . . We should therefore from every study or lesson gather up things brief and secure which we hide away in the little chest of our memory, from which later they may be drawn"; trans. Carruthers, *Craft*, 64.

59. Yet Augustine himself urged the futility of precise articulation of God. *Doctr. chr.* I.8 begins with the reservation: "Only they can think of God without absurdity who think of him as life itself [*vitam ipsam*]."

60. O'Donnell, *Augustine*, 107: privacy had "little or no meaning in St. Augustine's society." In order to avoid anachronistic use of "private" in discussing his practice of meditation, I will use the expression "Augustine *by himself,*" referencing Hannah Arendt's definition, "by himself," in Arendt, *Life of the Mind*, 185.

Meditation

The first task of meditation was to create a theme, or mental structure, that effectively cued and elicited memories, organizing discrete memories into parts of a whole. An adequate mental structure moved memories into relationships; so that memories that had seemed to be isolated from one another are remembered and gathered in.[61] The mental scheme that organized Augustine's self-understanding involved the actions of two agents, God's leading and Augustine's attentiveness, a cooperation or coordination he was still straining to describe in his last writings. On the one hand, God's grace does it all; on the other, humans play a necessary role—a true cooperation, not something one agent does to another.[62]

A further feature of medieval meditation owes a great deal to the influence of rhetoric on Augustine and to Augustine's influence.[63] *Ductus*, flow or motion, was a rhetorical concept indicating movement within and through the steps of a work's various parts. "*Ductus*, fueled by emotion, carries the self from one psychic place to another"; it is the journey that "guides a person to its various goals."[64] It is important to notice that these steps did not consist of a sequence of ideas or topics, but were rather "an affective, emotional route from fear to joy" informed, populated, by memories.[65]

Meditation had two primary characteristics: intense concentration and strong emotion. Emotion (*affectus*), the foundation of memory, prompted and supplied the energy for a meditative

---

61. Carruthers, *Craft*, 33–34, also 68–69: medieval monks "remembered" both "the invisible joys of paradise [and] the eternal torments of Hell" (quoting Boncampagno da Signa), constructing idea/pictures of these by collecting and collating scriptural suggestions, sense experience, and memories of emotions of bliss and pain.

62. St. Augustine's last communications still struggle to maintain an elusive balance between human will and God's action: *praed. sanct.* 3.7: "For these things are both commanded us and are shown to be God's gifts in order that we may understand both that we do them, and that God makes us to do them." *Praed. sanct.* 11.22; also *retr.* 1.23.3. See Burns, "Human Agency," 45–71.

63. Carruthers, *Craft*, 78.

64. Carruthers, *Craft*, 60.

65. Carruthers, *Craft*, 80.

Beautiful Bodies

withdrawal that "supplants food, sleep, and daily routines, blocking external stimuli."[66] In Western societies it has become commonplace to understand rationality as separate—and to be carefully sequestered—from emotion. We must jettison this modern assumption if we are to begin to understand St. Augustine, his contemporaries and his followers. Tears, the evidence of strong *feeling*, were considered essential to effective meditation. For the medieval monks studied by Mary Carruthers, Augustine's deathbed became the standard scenario for meditation: "lying prostrate and weeping 'in silence' (that is, in meditation)."[67]

St. Augustine's sermon on Psalm 6 emphasized that the function of tears in meditation is not merely to wash (*laudari*) but rather to cleanse or scour (*rigatio*) the soul. He specifies "a weeping that penetrates to the inside . . . weeping [that must reach] all the way to the innermost part of the heart."[68] Augustine remarked: "The holier a man is, and the fuller of holy desire, so much the more abundant is his weeping when he prays."[69] Carruthers comments: we cannot notice too strongly that "the impelling force, the energy for the journey, is emotional."[70]

---

66. Carruthers, *Book of Memory*, 200–201; "Both *strepitus* (noise) and *turba* (disturbance) are great mnemonic enemies."

67. Carruthers, *Craft*, 175. See also Van Fleteren et al., "Editorial Conclusions," 552. The editors describe "Augustine's enormous authority during the Christian Middle Ages. . . . All were followers of Augustine. To be Christian was to be Augustinian. Augustine was not in the mainstream; he defined the mainstream. . . . Augustine certainly was a 'founder' of medieval mysticism."

68. Andrée, "Tempus flendi," 185.

69. *Civ.* 10.17.

70. Carruthers, *Craft*, 103. The kind of emotions needed for meditation are not tranquil but "very strong emotions that both punctuated and wounded memory."

Augustine "by Himself"

> And men go abroad to wonder at the heights of mountains, the huge waves of the sea, the broad streams of rivers, the vastness of the ocean, the turnings of the stars—and they do not notice themselves.[71]

Augustine noticed himself: "Great indeed is the power of memory! It is something terrifying, my God, a profound and infinite multiplicity; and this thing is the mind, and this thing is I, myself [*et hoc ego ipse sum*]."[72] In *Confessions*, Augustine repeatedly referred to his youthful self as a heterogeneous mass of "spilled and scattered" memories: "and so it will be until all together I can flow into you, purified and molten by the power of your love ... and I shall stand and become set in you, formed in your truth."[73]

Only as a dying man did St. Augustine have the full narrative of his life, the memories in particular and specific detail, and the effective steps that could gel the scattered fragments of his experience into a *corpus*, a body, himself. And Augustine longed to see nothing less than himself, his life as formed and shepherded by God. His access to God's activity in his life was through memory: "I will go past this force of mine called memory; I will go beyond it so that I may draw nearer to you.... I mount up through my mind toward you who dwell above me ... for *I desire to reach you at the point from which you may be reached*."[74] His memories of God's agency in his life were the confident route by which Augustine approached God; in his memory, God's guidance could finally be *concretely* identified. St. Augustine had articulated this project, this desire, this longing, in *Confessions*; he completed it in the work of his deathbed tears.

---

71. *Conf.* 10.8.15; trans. Warner, *Confessions*, 219.
72. *Conf.* 10.17.26; trans. Warner, *Confessions*, 227, emphasis added.
73. *Conf.* 11.29–11.30.40; trans. Warner, *Confessions*, 283, slightly altered. Compare Plato, *Philebus* 1147e: Lacking organization of entities (such as memories), Plato said, "What you are bound to get ... is no real mixture, but literally a miserable mass of unmixed messiness."
74. *Conf.* 10.17.26 (emphasis added).

This urgent task required Augustine's memories, his rhetorical discipline, and—not least—his *affectus*, his *passio*. From this perspective it is not surprising that Augustine decided to stop work on *retr.* in order to complete the last sections of *doct. chr.*, sections that discussed rhetoric. For it was not only in his preaching and teaching that his training in rhetoric was useful; rhetoric also informed his meditation, the practice in which he found himself.[75]

The penitential psalms at which the dying Augustine gazed, weeping—(the earliest listing is from Cassiodorus in the sixth century)—Psalms 6, 31, 129, and 142, dramatize the steps of his meditative practice.[76] Each psalm begins with the psalmist's acknowledgment of extreme vulnerability, of physical and emotional suffering, and of frightening awareness of dangerous enemies. They plead for God's assistance. Each ends with confidence in, and gratitude for, God's love and mercy.

Possidius stated that Augustine's tears were penitential.[77] Clearly, we do not know what Possidius did not know, namely, the particular content of Augustine's tears. We can, however, gather Augustine's own descriptions of how he was accustomed to commune with his God from his meditative practice. Suggestions about the practice, process, and intent of his deathbed tears occur frequently, but not solely, in his last writings.[78]

---

75. Augustine's understanding of his self-identity as an individual, formed and shaped by God's inner leading, was significantly modified by his midlife revision of his primary identity as a participant in the body of Christ (discussed in Centerpiece). These self-understandings, however, are not mutually exclusive, nor are they necessarily sequential; they are complementary. Augustine's "self," designed by God's direction, was not annihilated, but realized—its isolation overcome—in the body of Christ.

76. Andrée, "Tempus flendi," 185; Grove, *Augustine on Memory*, 215; see also Grove's argument that Psalm 50 should be included in this list, in *Augustine on Memory*, 213-24.

77. Simon, *Postmodern Sexualities*, 153: "Intensity of feeling derives not from revealing ourselves to the other, but in revealing ourselves to ourselves." According to Freud, increments of self-knowledge always entail a "narcissistic wound," since they inevitably involve self-knowledge formerly repudiated and repressed. See Miles, "Augustine and Freud," 125.

78. *Ciu.* 20.17: "The holier a man is, and the fuller of holy desire, so much

In fact, Augustine had a long interest in developing effective meditative steps.[79] He refined his meditative practice throughout his Christian life, especially concerning the role of fear. An early treatise, *De quantitate animae* (*an. quant.*, written in 387–88 CE), lists seven steps, beginning with "the soul's care for its body," and culminating in "the vision and contemplation of truth." Only at step four does fear enter the process. Even then, fear plays no positive role; Augustine simply notes that fear brings the danger of "lessening that tranquility which is essential in the investigation of obscure matters." In *an. quant.* Augustine proposed alternative names for the steps in which it is clear that fear plays no role. These steps, he said, might also be described as: "beauty from another thing, beauty through another thing, beauty about another thing, beauty towards the beautiful, beauty in the beautiful, beauty towards beauty, [and] beauty in beauty."[80] Beauty became both the path and the goal of Augustine's early practice of meditation.

However, a decade later when he began to write *doctr. chr.* (begun in 396 CE), Augustine had changed his mind about the role of fear in meditation. The carefully plotted steps he described in his subsequent writings begin with strongly evoked fear. Augustine, a fearful man,[81] had learned the *use* of fear. Its essential importance is that it blocks pride: "Fear may inspire in us thought about our mortality and our inevitable future death, and, as our flesh begins to crawl [literally: breaks out in goose-flesh; *clauatis carnibus*], nails all our pride to the wood of the cross."[82]

---

the more abundant is his weeping when he prays" (trans. Dyson, *City of God*, 1004).

79. Ample evidence of Augustine's long interest in defining stages of ascent is provided in essays in Van Fleteren et al., *Augustine*, especially Teske, "St. Augustine," 287–308 for discussion of the steps Augustine outlined in *an. quant.* 33.70–76; and Tonna-Barthet, "Augustinian Mystical Theology," 558–65.

80. *An. quant.* 33.73; trans. Przywara, *Augustine Synthesis*, 26.

81. *Conf.* repeatedly states St. Augustine's fear of being laughed at, from readers' laughter (4.1.1; 1.9.14; 3.3.6; 10.12.19) to God's laughter (6.6.9).

82. *Doctr. chr.* 2.7.9, my translation. Carruthers *Craft*, 302n8, notes that *clauatis* is an unusual adjective, referring to "the prickly surfaces of the shells of some mollusks."

Beautiful Bodies

The second step is piety, by which we "believe that what is written [in Scripture] is more beneficial and more accurate than . . . what we can know of ourselves."[83] The third step is knowledge, which is "nothing else except that God must be loved for his own sake and our neighbor for the sake of God. . . . That is, that our entire love of our neighbor as also of ourselves is to be referred to God."[84] The fourth step is strength, the fifth mercy; the sixth step is cleansing "the eye of the heart," whereby God may be seen." "It is through these steps," Augustine wrote, "that we make our way to [the seventh step], to peace and tranquility."[85]

A late treatise, *The Gift of Perseverence* (*perseu.*, written in CE 428–29), affirms the usefulness of fear: "It is uncertain whether anyone has received the gift [of perseverance] as long as he is still alive." Considering this, Augustine noted, "It is good to fear."[86] Indeed, evoking fear in its full strength *fuels* the meditative journey. He said:

> Whoever does not want to fear, let him probe his inmost self. Do not just touch the surface; go down into yourself; reach into the farthest corner of your heart. Examine it with care: see there, whether a poisoned vein of the wasting love of the world still does not pulse, whether you are not moved by some physical desires, and are not caught in some law of the senses; whether you are never elated with empty boasting, never depressed by some vain anxiety; then only can you dare to announce that you are pure and crystal clear, when you have sifted everything in the deepest recesses of your inner being.[87]

---

83. *Doctr. chr.* 2.7.10; trans. Robertson, *On Christian Doctrine*, 39. Centuries later, Blaise Pascal commented similarly, "[T]he mystery furthest from our knowledge, that of the transmission of sin, [is] something without which we can have no knowledge of ourselves. . . . But for this mystery, the most incomprehensible of all, we remain incomprehensible to ourselves"; *Pensées* 1.7.131; trans. Krailsheimer, *Pensées*, 65.

84. *Doctr. chr.* 2.7.10; trans. Robertson, *On Christian Doctrine*, 39.

85. *Doctr. chr.* 2.7.11; trans. Robertson, *On Christian Doctrine*, 40.

86. *Perseu.* I.1; trans. Wallis, *Predestination*, 526.

87. *S.* 348.2.2; trans. Brown, *Augustine*, 432. Augustine described even the Last Judgment as a kind of self-judgment, based on memory. *Ciu.* 20.14; trans.

St. Augustine's Tears

In Augustine's later writings, fear is the first step in the meditative process; further steps both incorporate and transcend fear.[88] Augustine reiterated his meditative steps with slight variations in several late writings.[89] In *S*. 348, Augustine quoted Psalm 111.10, "The fear of the Lord is the beginning of wisdom," adding, "If you don't want to be afraid, learn how to fear."[90] He described steps that begin with fear, ascend through piety to knowledge, courage and mercy, to the cleansing of false values; together they lead to the seventh step, the "triumph of total security and peace in Christ." By "wending our way to God by these steps," he wrote, we climb to "a place of rest and peace."[91]

In short, Augustine's method of meditation consisted of carefully delineated steps, within a theme that effectively gathered from his memory substantial evidence of God's leading throughout his life, yielding something like a "God's eye view" of his life as a whole. No longer an abstraction, a narrative, or a matter of faith, on his deathbed, in his memory, God's leading "collapsed into immediacy."[92] The anxious neurasthenia of the young seeker has resolved in his experience—his memories—of God's guidance.

Augustine's long experience in meditation altered his description of the role of fear. As we have seen, early descriptions of his practice of meditation gave fear no role. In writings after 396 CE he insisted on the usefulness of fear, both as first step and

---

Dyson, *City of God*, 999: "Each one's knowledge will accuse or excuse his conscience, [so that] everyone will be judged simultaneously."

88. Augustine had learned how to use fear productively. Yet traces of anxiety remain. After Augustine sent Darius a copy of *Confessions*, he entreated him in *ep.* 231; trans. Parsons, *St. Augustine*, 163: "When you find me in these pages, pray for me . . . pray, my son, pray. I feel deeply what I am saying; I know what I am asking. . . . Let all who have learned to love me, pray for me . . . pray for me." *Ep.* 231 (c. 429 CE).

89. *S.* 348 3.4.

90. *Perseu.* 1.1.

91. *Perseu.* 6.12. Predestination is an "inscrutable" topic, one that must be left to God. "We live . . . more securely if we give the whole up to God, and do not entrust ourselves partly to him and partly to ourselves." Also *perseu.* 11.25: "God's ways, both in mercy and judgment, are past finding out."

92. The phrase is from Collingwood, *Idea of History*.

Beautiful Bodies

as the emotional energy that propels meditation. Shortly before his death, however, Augustine described the disappearance of fear: "Fear should grow less the closer we approach to our home country," he said, and "those who are arriving [will have] no fear at all."[93] "What has put fear out of the door [he said] is the love of God, whom you are loving with your whole heart and with your whole soul and with your whole mind."[94] Fear of death, formerly invoked so strongly as to cause flesh to prickle, has vanished. In the "valley of the shadow of death," St. Augustine reported, fear is cancelled by love. In short, fear has important but temporary uses, but love puts fear "out the door."

What about beauty? Did Augustine's reflections on the role of beauty in his search for God change since his powerful description of the role of beauty in his conversion? A decade before he wrote *Confessions,* Augustine, lover of beauty, had analyzed attentiveness to beauty as meditative steps. Later, in a closely reasoned sermon on the Gospel of John he said, "The way you are going is the same as the destination to which you are going."[95] Beauty, he suggested, can be both the way and the goal, the "beauty of all things beautiful."[96]

We must notice, however, that even though in mid-life he had understood that the beauty for which he longed was *only* to be found within, the images with which he pictured transcendent beauty were mediated, mysteriously transmogrified, through the senses: light, music, fragrance, embraces, food. It was only through his long practice of meditation that he learned to recognize God's activity *intus*, in his memory, in himself (*hoc est ipse sum*).

Yet there was a remarkable turn-about in Augustine's description of sensory beauty after he wrote *Confessions* In early writings he did not suggest that the beauty of human bodies should be included in gratitude for the beauty of creation. But in his discussion

93. *S.* 348.4; trans. Hill, *Sermons* III/10, 94.
94. *S.* 348.2; trans. Hill, *Sermons* III/10, 92.
95. *Io. eu. tr.* 13.4; my translation.
96. *Conf.* 3.6. By contrast, Plato's only treatise on beauty, *Greater Hippias* 1559e, *Dialogues,* explores the concept of beauty, coming to the inconclusive conclusion, "All that is beautiful is difficult."

of the resurrection in *ciu*. 22 (written c. 427 CE), Augustine described present human bodies as characterized essentially by the "harmonious congruence between all their parts and the beauty in their mutual arrangement and correspondence." Indeed, the beauty of bodies, "as we know them," he continued, makes it difficult or impossible to discern "whether the major factor in their creation was usefulness or beauty."[97] He gives multiple examples of the beauty of bodies, almost burying his point in detail; even the "internal organs, [he said], delight the mind with their rational beauty, having even greater beauty than the visible beauty of the external body."[98] In the resurrection, he wrote, bodies will no longer exist for backbreaking labor and painful childbearing, but *solely for beauty*.[99] In other words, in the resurrection, present bodies, "real bodies"—he insisted—relieved of their "uses," will be "reduced"[100] to their essence, beauty:

> If now, in such great fragility of the flesh and in such weak operation of our members, such great beauty of body appears that it entices the passionate and stimulates the learned to investigate . . . how much more beautiful will the body be there where there will be no distracting lust (*illicit libidinosis*), no corruption, no unsightly deformity, no miserable necessity, but instead unending eternity, beautiful truth, and utmost happiness.[101]

97. *Ciu*. 22.24; trans. Dyson, *City of God*, 1163.

98. *Ciu*. 22.24; trans. Dyson, *City of God*, 1163.

99. *Ciu*. 22.24; trans. Dyson, *City of God*, 1163. Moreover, when "not a few" Christians were saying that the promised perfection of body meant that women will be given male bodies in the resurrection, Augustine insisted that female bodies are not part of the punishment of the human race, but are, like male bodies, the good creation of God, and thus will be retained in the resurrection. This passage was discussed in the Preface as informing Signorelli's "Resurrection of the Flesh" in the San Brizio Chapel, Orvieto Cathedral.

100. "*Reductio*" in medieval usage signified boiling a sauce to its essence without taking out any of its ingredients as, for example, in St. Boaventure's *The Reduction of the Arts to Theology*.

101. S. 243.8.7; my translation. The seventeenth-century English divine Thomas Traherne wrote: "We love we know not what and therefore everything allures us," in *Centuries of Meditation* 1.2.

Beautiful Bodies

Beautiful bodies became, for the old Augustine, urgent and vivid testimony to the beauty and generosity of their creator.

At the time of his death, Augustine knew who he was before God, and he insisted on dying as that man, not as seeker, not as pastor or bishop, or as defender of doctrine. In mid-life he identified the primary story of his life. He began to construct this narrative in *conf.*, but he completed it on his deathbed when he was at last in possession of the full wealth of detailed memories that gave flesh to the narrative. Augustine offered his own practice of meditation as evidence that as love becomes capacious, meditation is no longer pushed, energized, and propelled by fear, but is attracted, drawn, pulled as by a magnet, by emotions no less strong: gratitude, peace, beauty, and love. Praise was the vocabulary—the activity—of profound gratitude. St. Augustine's deathbed tears were richly complex: penitential certainly, but he was also powerfully moved by seeing his life as a whole, by recognizing God's utterly trustworthy leading in "*both* the bad and the good that I did."[102] And the beauty was overwhelming.

---

102. Based on his reading of Augustine's mid-life "shift from self to whole," Grove persuasively interprets Augustine's deathbed tears as informed by his primary self-identity as communal, as body of Christ, "becoming Christ," in *Augustine on Memory*, 225–26.

Chapter Five

Resurrected Bodies

Perfect health of body will be the ultimate immortality of the whole person.
(*Ep.* 118.3.14)

WRITING *THE CITY OF GOD*, in the last years of his life, Augustine often addressed the Platonist Porphyry (d. 305 CE), whom he referred to as "the greatest philosopher and the greatest enemy of Christians."[1] Porphyry, who was said to have once been a Christian "denied the resurrection of all bodies as absurd." He taught that "the body of Christ and all other bodies must be left behind at death to perish and dissolve." There could be no possibility of "the soul's returning to its original body in any condition."[2] Augustine

---

1. A curiously mixed compliment; it is almost as if Augustine could not help admiring Porphyry's critical perspicacity in attacking the doctrine simultaneously most indispensable to Christian belief and practice *and* most uncomfortably mystifying to believers.
2. *Ciu.* 10.29. O'Meara, *Porphyry's Philosophy*, 77.

asserted that Porphyry's "flee all bodies" (*omne corpus fugiendum*) was formulated specifically to oppose Christian teaching on the resurrection of bodies. Augustine thought him to be "the greatest enemy of Christians," not because Porphyry did not believe, but because he fulminated against the *very* doctrine Christians themselves found most difficult to believe.

Augustine agreed with Porphyry that the bodily resurrection was indeed the most baffling—counterintuitive, daring, and "unbelievable"—Christian doctrine. Yet the bodily resurrection is essential to Christian belief, supported as it is by scriptural witness to Jesus's resurrection. Although Augustine repeatedly urged others to *believe* doctrines they cannot (as yet) understand, he was not himself content with this admonition; he struggled patiently to understand over a period of many years. The resurrection of body was such a doctrine; he *affirmed* it from his earliest writings, but it was not until his last few years that he *understood*—with the delight that marked his late sermons—body's centrality to Christian belief.

Augustine recognized the doctrine's difficulty "from his own experience,"[3] of struggle to make it conceptually accessible. In his early writings, his rhetorical skill at identifying familiar analogies based on present experience did not help. He did not, however, consider the difficulty a reason to reject, or even to minimize, the doctrine. Rather than sidelining it, Augustine made it the centerpiece of his theology,

> For the sake of praising God . . . we cannot remain silent as to the joy of our hope . . . how great will be that joy, which we certainly have no power to describe, because we have not yet experienced it.[4]

In Augustine's education, the philosophical consensus was unanimous that a positive appreciation of body was an obstacle to "getting your mind right." In the light of classical Platonism, the prospect of being "stuck" in the vulnerable body of present

3. *Conf.* 8.5.
4. *Ciu.* 20.19; 22.21.

experience was horrific.[5] Throughout his vocation as bishop and preacher, Augustine knew that he must defend this doctrine, not only against critics, but also for the benefit of Christians who found it incredible. Concluding *ciu.* (books 18–22, 425–27 CE), Augustine was still defending the doctrine of the resurrection of all human beings to immortal reward or punishment as he had from his earliest writings. It was in *ciu.* and in his last sermons that he demonstrated he had arrived with confidence and delight at the perfect metaphor for the resurrection of body.

Each chapter in this volume has explored a significant change in Augustine's thinking on a subject of importance to living as a Christian. Together they demonstrate a life committed to learning, together with a commitment to the humility requisite to learning. As a young man, he despaired of recognizing him*self* without sex; he was, in his own strong words, a "slave to lust" (*libidinous seruus*).[6] His *Confessions* narrate his laborious tracing of his bondage, the last stronghold to be relinquished with anguish as he chose celibacy. His *Confessions* find God's unerring leading *within* his captivity, in his tale of "disorder and early sorrow."[7] However, in middle age, as he preached on the psalms, his self-identity shifted to understanding him*self,* intimately and essentially, as a member of the body of Christ, embedded in the "whole Christ."[8] In old age, his understanding of bodies had further evolved from abstract (philosophical) to substantial, personal, and intimate; the old Augustine carefully described the *continuities and discontinuities* of present and future embodied life. Augustine's revised identity as a member of the body of Christ affected his idea of the bodily resurrection. Just as his concept of identity changed from *focus* on the

---

5. Barnes, *Elizabeth Finch*, 99: Platonists found the Christian doctrine of the general resurrection of the body "not only absurd but disgusting—the notion that we shall be forever saddled with our bodies, down to the last corn, cataract, and bunion." Augustine's *S.* 213.9 responded: "Do not shudder at the resurrection of the body. See its good aspects, forget the bad . . . whatever bodily complaints there are now will not exist then."

6. *Conf.* 6.13.

7. The title of a short story by Thomas Mann.

8. Grove, *Augustine on Memory*, 8; discussed in Centerpiece.

individual without erasing individuals, so his idea of bodily resurrection encompassed both individual and corporate resurrection. In the resurrection as presently, individuality is not absorbed without a trace in the body of Christ, but completed and perfected.[9]

Throughout these chapters I have suggested that Augustine was concerned not only to support the testimony of Scripture and tradition but also with the *effect* of particular doctrines on Christian life *now*. This chapter explores the relevance of Augustine's understanding of the doctrine of the resurrection of bodies to present Christian life. Following the plan of earlier chapters, in the "conditions of this life," as Augustine said—that is, with inadequate time to detail evidence of his changing esteem of bodies—I will compare his earliest comments on the value of bodies, with his last discussion, several years before his death.

Augustine's Early Theology of Resurrection

In an early treatise, *De quantitate animae* (387–88 CE), Augustine endeavored to "normalize" the bodily resurrection by comparing it to the everyday recurrence of the dawn:

> We shall also see that the corporeal nature, in obedience to the divine law, undergoes so many changes and vicissitudes that we may hold even the resurrection of the body... to be so certain that the rising of the sun, after it has gone down, is not more certain to us.[10]

Clearly, the analogy is flawed; sunrises *set* at the end of the day and appear the following morning. But the doctrine's claim is not that resurrected bodies will come and go—again and again—but that resurrected bodies will never die.

Another early treatise (roughly contemporary with *Confessions*), *De musica* (387–91 CE), takes a more philosophical

---

9. Grove, *Augustine on Memory*, 222, 224.

10. *An. quant.* 23.76. It is difficult to know how to interpret this early statement as, a few lines later, Augustine wrote: "Death... the flight and escape from this body, is now yearned for as the greatest boon."

approach. Augustine undertook an ambitious intellectual exercise in demonstrating that Pythagorean music theory can be applied to understanding time (rhythm) and creation (motion). He considered the relative value of body and soul, seeking to remedy philosophers' disdain for body by insisting on a place for body within a hierarchy of values. He understood that the doctrines of creation, Jesus's incarnation, and the resurrection of body all insistently value human bodies as integral to human beings: "for the body also is a creature of God and is adorned in its own beauty, *although of the lowest kind.*"[11]

> The body the soul used to animate and govern ... [was] changed for the worse by the first sin [and made] subject to death and corruption. ... Yet, it has a beauty of its own, and in this way it sets its dignity off to fair advantage in the eyes of the soul.[12]

De musica was Augustine's *tour de force,* a brilliant young man's intellectual demonstration of the compatibility of Christian teaching, rhetoric, and music theory, an effort to synthesize Christianity with his education. He concluded his discussion with an axiom he repeated many times in treatises and sermons: "It's not those numbers below reason and beautiful in their kind [that] soil the soul, but the *love* of lower beauty."[13] At this time, Augustine's philosophical interest in human bodies was *abstract,* but he already understood that *because of their beauty,* human bodies cannot be simply ignored.

In *Confessions,* roughly contemporaneous with *mus.,* Augustine described his first step toward understanding the significance of created entities. Seeking knowledge of God, he asked the "blowing breezes, the creeping things, the heaven, moon, and stars ... what is this God?" They unanimously responded, "we are not your God ... [but] He made us." Augustine observed, "My question was in my contemplation of them, and *their answer was in their*

---

11. *An. quant.* 6.14.46.
12. *Mus.* 6.33.76.
13. *Mus.* 6.13.39.

Beautiful Bodies

beauty."[14] Augustine recognized a connection that would continue to be central to his mature understanding of the bodily resurrection, namely, the *theological significance* of beauty as the mark of its creator. The link between God and created things is the indelible mark of "the most beautiful, the creator of beauty in all things."[15]

Although he recognized created entities as "creatures of God," he did not yet *apply this insight to human bodies*. Instructed by Christian doctrines, but stuck within the conceptual universe of his philosophical training, his early writings depend on his inherited system of higher and lower entities. Before he could picture the bodily resurrection, he must extend his insight that the beauty of creation reveals the beauty of its creator.

Seeking knowledge of God, Augustine considered his own body and soul, quickly finding—as his education had taught him to expect—that "the interior [higher] part of me is the better."[16] Here he finds "the life of [my] life," but, he reflects, animals too have life. He has not yet identified the place in which God acts. He goes on to examine memory, which he considered the uniquely *human* feature of himself.[17] But *all* humans have memory. Much more significant for Augustine is that memory is a unique collection of *his* memories, defining *his* individuality. This is the place of God's activity, he decided.[18]

Fortified by his identification of the site of God's activity, Augustine sorted through his memories, even those memories that "have been swallowed up and buried in forgetfulness."[19] Preceding active memory, he had "imbibed the name of Christ with his

---

14. *Conf.* 10.6; emphasis added.

15. *Conf.* 1.7. Also *conf.* 3.6, "the beauty of all things beautiful"; 10.6, "beauty, so old and so new."

16. *Conf.* 10.6.10.

17. Memory is the "stomach [*uenter*] of the mind"; *conf.*, 10.14.21; trans. Warner, *Confessions*, 223.

18. *Conf.* 9.5, emphasis added; trans. Warner, *Confessions*, 191: "It was *there, there* in the place where I had been angry with myself, inside, in my own room, *there* where I had been pierced . . . *there* it was that you began to grow sweet to me."

19. *Conf.* 10.8.

(Christian) mother's milk."[20] Surveying the "vast fields" of memory, Augustine noticed that memory stores not only experiences and ideas, but also "the feelings of my mind."[21] Considering feelings an essential ingredient of thinking, he scrutinized his feelings as he recounted the occasions of greatest significance in his life, consistently examining his feelings as fully and carefully—if not more so—as his decisions and their rationale.

In brief, instructed by Christian doctrines of creation, the incarnation, and the resurrection of bodies, yet boxed within the conceptual universe of higher and lower, he maintained the value of body, but considered body the lowest of God's creations. Resurrected bodies continued to both fascinate and frustrate him until he replaced his understanding of human beings as composed of higher and lower features.

The Old Augustine

In old age, the occasions, circumstances, feelings, and thoughts—the richness—of a lifetime can be gathered, revisited, and experienced again in memory. The wealth of a life, fully lived, the "bad and good,"[22] together with the learnings, are now known, a vantage point inaccessible in earlier periods of life. Even one's education, inadequate as it may have been, can now be acknowledged as the source of ideas that are woven into one's long perspective. Augustine's education, strongly influenced by Platonism, returned furtively but confidently, throughout his life in his recognition of beauty, not an intellectual judgment, but *as a feeling* of pleasurable excitement. As both Plato and Plotinus insisted, the presence of beauty prompts an unmistakable *feeling*. We cannot define beauty, Plato observed, but *we know it when we feel it*.[23] In old age,

20. *Conf.* 1.6.
21. *Conf.* 10.14: "affectiones animi mei."
22. *Retr.* 2.6.
23. Plato, Phaedrus 251a–e; trans. Hackforth, *Collected Dialogues*, 497–98: "When someone sees a godlike face or a bodily form that truly expresses beauty, there comes upon him shuddering and awe . . . next, with the passing of

Beautiful Bodies

Augustine also understood that beauty plays an essential theological role; it is beauty that *connects* present human bodies—described by Plato as the "frailer loveliness of flesh and blood"[24]—with the beautiful bodies of the resurrection.

What follows is a foreshortened summary of Augustine's long process of imagining the resurrection of bodies. Augustine realized incrementally that the present human body is more than a metaphor; indeed, it is a *link* to the resurrection body. Augustine's recognition exemplifies his theological method, which Grove called "first order theology"; namely, in sermons he introduced and explored insights that he later developed more systematically in treatises.[25]

Augustine stated that bodies will then (*tunc*) be spirit but, he insisted, they will still be flesh. The present experience of a tug-of-war between spirit and flesh will not characterize resurrection bodies. They will be capable of enjoying fleshly pleasures—with a difference: resurrected bodies will eat and sleep (Augustine's examples) for pleasure, rather than, as now (*nunc*), for necessary maintenance.

"How wonderful will body's condition be, when it will, in every way, be subject to the spirit, by which it will be made *so fully alive* as to need no other nourishment!"[26]

---

the shudder, a strange sweating and seizure seizes him . . . for by reason of the stream of beauty entering his eyes there comes a warmth. . . . [The soul] throbs with ferment in every part; it throbs like a fevered pulse . . . perplexed and frenzied." Plotinus, *Ennead* 1.6.4; trans. Armstrong, *Plotinus*, 245: "There must be those who see this beauty . . . and when they see it they must be delighted and overwhelmed and excited. . . . These experiences must occur whenever there is contact with any sort of beautiful thing, wonder, and a shock of delight and longing and passion, and a happy excitement. . . . He who sees them cannot say anything except that they are what really exists. What does 'really exist' mean? That they exist as beauties."

24. Plato, *Symposium* 211e; trans. Michael Joyce, *Symposium*, 563.

25. Grove, *Augustine on Memory*, 8: In sermons, Augustine "conjures up ideas, develops and refines them, and then revisits them. His most extraordinary discoveries emerge in his sermons and radiate outward" into his treatises.

26. *Ciu.* 22.24.

> Anyone who interprets this in such a way as to think that the earthly body as we have it now is so changed into a spiritual body at the resurrection that there will be neither these members nor the substance of flesh is ... certainly to be reproved, instructed by the body of the Lord who, after the resurrection, appeared with the same members.[27]

How did Augustine's midlife relinquishment of his earlier self identity, as an individual formed by God's leading, affect his hypothetical picture of resurrected bodies? According to Augustine, the resurrection of bodies will be both individual and corporate. He explained that "perfect man" refers to Christ's body, the church: "the body of Christ and his members ... we being many are one bread, one body."[28] Individuality is not absorbed without trace in the "body of Christ," but completed and perfected.

Many quotations from sermons document his fundamentally altered *perspective*. First, responding to criticism that he was too strict in requiring his cadre of clergy to live in poverty, Augustine said: "Let me have a loss of [great merit] here so I can enter the kingdom of heaven *with all of you*."[29] This was not a philosophical statement, nor that of a proud young professor of rhetoric. It was, rather, the moving confession of an old priest who deeply loved fellow members of the body of Christ. The following poignant quotation is from a very late sermon (dated 425–30 CE):

> What, after all, do I want? What do I desire? What am I longing for? Why am I speaking? Why am I sitting here? What do I live for, if not with this intention that we should all live together with Christ? That is my desire, that is my honor, that is my most treasured possession,

---

27. *Retr.* 1.16.

28. *Ciu.* 22.17–18, 24; trans. Dyson, *City of God*, 1144–46, 1164. Since "not a few" believe that women will be assigned male bodies in the resurrection, becoming, as promised, "perfect man," Augustine said that he preferred the "better opinion," namely, that "the woman is the creation of God, just as the man is," and therefore will retain her sex in the resurrection. What *will* disappear is the old 'uses,' namely, debilitating labor, sexual intercourse [since the human race will not need to be repopulated], and painful childbearing.

29. *S.* 356.15; trans. Hill, *Sermons* III/10, 181.

that is my joy, my pride and glory. I don't want to be saved without you.[30]

Far from being the words of an "incoherent," or "rambling" old man, Augustine's feeling is eloquently and precisely expressed. In such sermonic moments, hearers (and readers) see the once-young professor of rhetoric at his best, "aged to perfection" like a fine wine.[31] Augustine characterized his "loving concern" for fellow members of Christ's body as "that of a mother as well as a father" (*s.* 361.4).[32]

> By the time of sermons CCXL through CCXLIII—between 418-20 CE—Augustine recognized and developed the implications of the human body itself as the experiential metaphor for the resurrection body. His metaphor for the resurrection has moved from the distant analogy of the rising sun to the intimate human experience of embodiment.[33]

Beautiful Bodies

In *ciu.* 22 Augustine walked his readers through his own process of recognition of body's centrality to Christian faith.[34] First, he noted that human bodies are erect, "facing toward heaven, not facing the earth like animals." Next, he remarked on the "wonderful mobility

---

30. S. 17.2.

31. See chapter 3 n. 33 for evidence of *ageism* (as a settled perspective) in a volume of translations of Augustine's sermons. Why is "aged to perfection" understood as a high compliment when referring to wine, but it is not said of a human being?!

32. As a youth, Augustine experienced his mother's care as persistently and annoyingly directive; later, however, he thought of her as the "voice of God" to him (*conf.* 9.10).

33. Miles, *Augustine on the Body*, 115.

34. It is important not to conflate Augustine's account of sex before the Fall (*ciu.* 14.26) with his description of resurrected bodies. The situations differ; reproduction of the human race was necessary before the Fall, but will not be needed in the resurrection.

with which the tongue and hands are equipped" making possible speech, writing, and all the arts. Indeed, the "harmonious congruence of body parts creates such beauty that it is hard to see whether the major factor in their creation was usefulness or beauty."[35] Even the "useful" parts of the body are beautiful. His thought interrupted by spontaneous delight, he paused to address Porphyry's objection to the doctrine of the resurrection of bodies: "What is required to ensure the soul's blessedness is not an escape from any kind of body whatsoever, but the acquisition of an incorruptible body." Checking his enthusiasm, Augustine continued, conceding once again that body's afterlife resurrection is difficult to believe. As he had written almost forty years before, it must be "believed before it is fully understood."[36] He acknowledged that "imperishable bodies"—bodies that do not contain a built-in timed trajectory of growth and dissolution—are so foreign to present experience that they are difficult to imagine:

> No experience that we have yet had enables us to know what the nature of that spiritual body and the extent of its grace will be; and so it would, I fear, be rash to offer any description of it. . . . [Nevertheless] for the sake of praising God we cannot remain silent.[37]

Appropriately daunted but undeterred by the difficulty of belief, he ventured a hypothetical picture of resurrected bodies. In fact, he realized, we actually *can* "get there from here" (conceptually); in the beauty of present bodies, the beauty of resurrected bodies can be glimpsed.

> If now (nunc), in such frailty of the flesh and in such weak operation of our members, such great beauty of body appears that it entices the passionate and stimulates the learned and the thoughtful to investigate it . . . *how much more beautiful will the body be then* (tunc) where there will be no lust (libidinosus), no corruption, no unsightly

---

35. *Ciu.* 22.24.
36. *Mus.* 6.13.
37. *Ciu.* 22.21.

Beautiful Bodies

deformity, no miserable necessity, but instead unending eternity, beautiful truth, and utmost happiness.[38]

At this point, it would seem that Augustine might well urge his hearers to "leave it to God," rather than attempt further to picture resurrected bodies. He did not suggest this, however, because he recognized two reasons to imagine the beauty of resurrection bodies. First, as already mentioned, he was a pastor, dedicated to helping his congregation to believe. This is the Augustine who patiently speculated on a volley of questions of wildly uneven importance in correspondence and, I imagine, at the basilica door following a service. In long passages in the closing books of *ciu.*, Augustine also does his best to respond to obscure curious questions; rarely did he simply acknowledge helpless ignorance. But he found it even more important to reassure and comfort those mourning the loss of beloved family members than to speculate about the details of resurrected bodies.

It must be acknowledged that Augustine did not picture resurrected bodies in the colorful individuality of his friends depicted in *Confessions*. He envisioned them, rather, *as seen by loving eyes*. Augustine the pastor comforted the consecrated virgin, Sapida, as she mourned her brother's death. His letter to her[39] assured her that, although she presently grieves, she will see him again on the day of resurrection. But Augustine suspected that this reassurance was too distant to comfort her, so he urged Sapida to recall her sensory experience of her brother in order to "remember" his resurrected body.[40]

> That body through which he was visible to you, through which he spoke to you and conversed with you, through which his voice issued forth as well known to you as is his face, so that he was always recognized to you though

---

38. *S.* 243.8; *Ep.* 118.3.14 (emphasis added).

39. *Ep.* 263.

40. As the medieval monks studied by Mary Carruthers "remembered" the joys of paradise and the torments of hell "by collecting and collating scriptural suggestions, sense experience, and memories of bliss and pain," in *Craft*, 33–34, 68–69.

not seen, whenever you heard his voice . . . they will be restored so as never again to be laid aside, but changed for the better and made strong.[41]

Emotional support was a high priority for Augustine. Even as he argued the fundamental "inscrutability" of predestination in *The Predestination of the Saints* (428–29 CE), he did not neglect to address the pain of bereavement. He quoted Cyprian's treatise, *On Mortality*: "A great number of those who are dear to us are expecting us there, a dense and abundant crowd of parents, sisters and brothers, and daughters and sons are longing for us."[42]

Second, Augustine imagined resurrected bodies in order to activate and stimulate *hope* for that life.[43] The occupation of the elect in eternal life will be never-wearying *praise* of God, a vocation for which Augustine trained his voice in this life, whether writing his confessions[44] or preaching to his congregation.

Augustine discovered that present bodies *do*, after all, offer a strong hint about resurrected bodies. *Resurrected bodies will be beautiful*. His most frequently quoted verse in writings and sermons was 1 Cor 13:2, employing the syncrisis: *nunc . . . tunc* to indicate continuity of experience across antithetical terms: "We see now through a glass darkly; then however, face to face." Bodies, whether present (*nunc*) or resurrected (*tunc*), are beautiful. Beginning in *Confessions*, with the beauty of creation, the young Augustine recognized that created entities, whether skies or trees, oceans or birds, inevitably reflect the beauty "so old and so new" of their creator.[45] From that realization, although much later, he noticed

---

41. *Ep.* 263; trans. Parsons, *St. Augustine*.

42. *Praed. sanct.* 28.

43. Augustine described the eternal suffering of the damned in similar detail. I may wish he had been content to "leave it to God." Nevertheless, bound by Scripture and tradition, his exposition on the miseries of the damned must be respected. It does seem, however, that if he sought to inspire fear and repentance by this painful feat of the imagination, his effort seems to contradict the doctrine of predestination, which declares the question of one's eternal destiny fixed and incontrovertible.

44. *Conf.* 1.1.

45. *Conf.* 10.6.

Beautiful Bodies

the beauty of "God's greatest creation," human bodies. Startlingly, in several sermons he said that human birth is a greater miracle than Jesus's resurrection.[46]

Augustine might even have observed that we don't need to *believe* in beauty; we have *seen* it in present bodies! But perhaps someone has not noticed the beauty of present bodies.[47] If one has *seen and noticed* the beauty of present human bodies, however, it is a short step to imagine the beauty of resurrected bodies, marked, like present bodies, by the beauty of their creator.

In old age, Augustine "*fleshed out*" the bodily resurrection for his hearers and readers. "This flesh will rise, this flesh which is buried, which dies, this flesh which is felt, which is touched."[48] In spite of his repeated acknowledgment that it would be "rash" to speculate about resurrection bodies, he did so with excitement and obvious pleasure. "For the sake of praising God," he imagined how the bodily resurrection will look and feel.

> All the limbs and organs of the body, no longer subject to decay, the parts which we now see assigned to various essential functions, will then be freed from all such constraint, since full, secure, certain, and eternal felicity will have displaced necessity; and all those parts will contribute to the praise of God. For even those elements in the bodily harmony . . . the harmonies which, in our present state are hidden, will then be hidden no longer. Dispersed internally and externally, through-out the whole body, and combined with other great and marvelous things that will then be revealed, they will kindle our

---

46. S. 126.4; trans. Hill, *Sermons* III/4, 271.

47. Lacking Augustine's own words, I presume to suggest that *concupiscentia* (lust) blinds the eye to the beauty of bodies of all ages, all skin colors, and all abilities. The aggressive, acquisitive eye seeks to possess its object (voyeuristically/sexually), rather than to enjoy for its own sake the remarkable created beauty of bodies. Isn't the overdub of lust what Augustine described in his *Confessions* of his youthful *concupiscentia*? This suggestion might be (negatively) supported by the significant lack of any reference to physical beauty in Augustine's sexual partners.

48. S. 264.4.

minds to the praise of the great artist by the delight afforded by a beauty that satisfies reason.[49]

St. Augustine's theological loyalties were to Scripture and tradition; the urgency with which he preached and wrote, I have suggested, were the result of his concerns about *present life*. How did the doctrines of predestination and perseverance affect present life? As discussed in chapter 3, these doctrines effectively remove the possibility that persons can, in any way—by behavior or pleading—affect their eternal destination, which was decided "before the foundations of the world." "Leave it to God," Augustine said of these doctrines; don't speculate on "inscrutable matters."[50] Nevertheless, these "inscrutable matters" are declared, if not explained, in Scripture, and he pondered their possible meanings. Augustine interpreted these doctrines as firmly closing human access to the God who predestines. They would seem to be of little or no usefulness for present Christian life. Yet Augustine understood their benefit to be enormous; namely they prevent pride and require humility.

The God who predestines individuals to reward or punishment is not the aspect of God-is-love who is *with* Christians, intimately (*intus*) guiding and sustaining them as they "walk along the road: "one is not only instructed so as to see you [God], but also so as to grow strong enough so as to hold (*teneat*) you, and the one who cannot see you for the distance may yet walk along the road by which he will arrive and see you and hold you."[51] Humility is the posture that enables learning, which Augustine called "walking along the road."[52] Walking in humility replaced the young Augustine's confident expectation that he would arrive, in this life, at the serenity and authoritative status of a philosopher or apostle.[53]

When he preached, St. Augustine longed not primarily to *convince*, but to prompt—to trigger—the *experience that is belief,*

---

49. *Ciu.* 22.30.
50. *Perseu.* 11.25.
51. *Conf.* 7.21.
52. *Io. eu. tr.* 54.8.
53. Brown, "The Lost Future," in *Augustine*, chapter 15.

to elicit the sudden, spontaneous *feeling* that reason, no matter how persuasive, is powerless to generate. The feeling of God's love, circulating lavishly among companions in the body of Christ, is the embodied experience Augustine sought to rouse as he preached, in earnest of the fully alive bodies—bodies undiluted by mortality—of the day of resurrection. This body is nothing less than the familiar, intimately known body (*nunc*), united with, and inseparable from, "life itself" (*tunc*).[54]

In short, the doctrine of the resurrection of body articulates and responds to "the deepest human feeling."

> I know you want to keep on living. You do not want to die. And you want to pass from this life to another in such a way that you will not rise again as a dead person, but fully alive and transformed. This is what you desire. *This is the deepest human feeling*: mysteriously, the soul itself wishes and instinctively desires it.[55]

---

54. *Doct. chr.* 1.8.
55. *S.* 344.4; trans. Hill, *Sermons* III/10, 51 (emphasis added).

Translations Cited

Abbreviations

FC   Fathers of the Church

NCP   New City Press

NPNF Nicene Post Nicene Fathers

Armstrong, A. H. *Plotinus, The Enneads*. Vol. 1. Loeb Classical Library 440. Cambridge: Harvard University Press, 1966.
Bogan, Mary Inez, RSM. *The Retractions*. FC 60. New York: Catholic University of America Press, 1968.
Boulding, Maria, OSB. *Essential Expositions of the Psalms*. The Works of St. Augustine. New York: NCP, 2015.
———. *Expositions of the Psalms III*. The Works of St. Augustine. New York: NCP, 2015.
Burleigh, J. H. S. *St. Augustine, Of True Religion*. Chicago: Henry Regnery, 1968.
———. *To Simplicianus, On Various Questions*. Book 1. Augustine: Early Writings. Philadelphia: Westminster, 1953.
Burnaby, John. *The Spirit and the Letter*. Augustine: Later Works. Philadelphia: Westminster, 1954.
———. *Ten Homilies on the First Epistle of St. John*. Augustine: Later Works. Philadelphia: Westminster, 1955.
Defarrari, Mary E. *Eight Questions of Dulcitius*. FC 16. New York: Catholic University of America Press, 1952.
Dyson, R. W. *The City of God against the Pagans*. Cambridge: Cambridge University Press, 1998.
Fairweather, A. M. *Aquinas on Nature and Grace*. The Library of Christian Classics. Philadelphia: Westminster, 1954.

Translations Cited

Gilligan, Thomas F., OSA. *Soliloquies*. FC 5. New York: Catholic University of America Press, 1948.

Great Books of the Western World. Vol. XXXI. Chicago: Encyclopedia Britannica, 1952.

Hackforth, R. *Phaedrus*. In *The Collected Dialogues of Plato*, edited by Edith Hamilton and Huntington Cairns. New York: Princeton University Press, 1962.

Hill, Edmund OP. *Homilies on the Gospel of John, 1–40*. The Works of Saint Augustine: A Translation for the 21st Century. New York: NCP, 2020.

———. *Homilies on the Gospel of John, 41–194*. The Works of Saint Augustine: A Translation for the 21st Century. New York: NCP, 2020.

———. *Sermons III/1*. The Works of Saint Augustine: A Translation for the 21st Century. New York: NCP, 1990.

———. *Sermons III/3*. The Works of Saint Augustine: A Translation for the 21st Century. New York: NCP, 1991.

———. *Sermons III/4*. The Works of Saint Augustine: A Translation for the 21st Century. New York: NCP, 1992.

———. *Sermons III/5*. The Works of Saint Augustine: A Translation for the 21st Century. New York: NCP, 1992.

———. *Sermons III/10*. The Works of Saint Augustine: A Translation for the 21st Century. New York: NCP, 1995.

Huegelmeyer, Charles T. *Adulterous Marriages*. FC 27. New York: Catholic University of America Press, 1955.

Joyce, Michael. *Symposium*. In *The Collected Dialogues of Plato*, edited by Edith Hamilton and Huntington Cairns. New York: Princeton University Press, 1962.

Krailsheimer, A. J. *Pensées*. Baltimore, MD: Penguin, 1966.

McKenna, Stephen, CSSR. *St. Augustine: The Trinity*. Fathers of the Church Patristic Series. Washington, DC: Catholic University of America Press, 1963.

Meagher, Luanne, OSB. *The Advantage of Believing*. FC 2. New York: Catholic University of America Press, 1947.

Mourant, John A., and William Collinge. *Four Anti-Pelagian Writings*. FC 86. New York: 1992.

Murray, J. C., SJ. *Admonition and Grace*. FC. 2. New York: Catholic University of America Press, 1947.

Paolucci, Henri. *St. Augustine: The Enchiridion on Faith, Hope, and Love*. Chicago: Regnery, 1961.

Parsons, Wilfrid, SND. *St. Augustine: Letters*. FC 32. New York: Catholic University of America Press, 1956.

Peebles, Bernard M. *Faith, Hope, and Charity*. FC 2. New York: Catholic University of America Press, 1947.

Plato. *The Collected Dialogues of Plato*. Edited by Edith Hamilton and Huntington Cairns. Bollingen Series LXXI. New York: Princeton University Press, 1962.

Translations Cited

Przywara, Erich. *An Augustine Synthesis*. New York: Harper, 1958.
Ramsey, Boniface. *Revisions*. Vol. 1/2. The Works of Saint Augustine: A Translation for the 21st Century. New York: NCP, 2010.
Robertson, D. W. *On Christian Doctrine*. New York: Bobbs-Merrill, 1958.
Russell, Robert, OSA. *Faith and the Creed*. FC 27. New York: Catholic University of America Press, 1955.
Schopp, Ludwig. *The Happy Life*. FC 5. New York: Catholic University of America Press, 1948.
Taliaferro, Robert Catesby. *On Music*. FC 2. New York: Catholic University of America Press, 1947.
Teske, Roland J. *Answer to the Pelagians*. Vol. 1/23. The Works of Saint Augustine: A Translation for the 21st Century. New York: NCP, 1997.
———. *Letters*. Vol. II/2. The Works of Saint Augustine: A Translation for the 21st Century. New York: NCP, 2002.
Wallis, R. E. *The Predestination of the Saints*. NPNF 5. Buffalo, NY: Christian Literature Publishing, 1887.
Walsh, P. G. *Augustine: De Bono Coniugali, De sancta Uirginitate*. Oxford: Clarendon, 2001.
Warner, Rex. *The Confessions of St. Augustine*. New York: Mentor, 1963.
Weiskotten, Herbert T. *Possidius: The Life of St. Augustine*. Merchantville, NJ: Evolution, 2008.
Zimmerman, Odo John, OSB. *Dialogues of Saint Gregory the Great I*. FC 39. New York: Catholic University of America Press, 1959.

Bibliography

Andrée, Alexander. "Tempus flendi et tempus ridendi." In *Tears, Sighs, and Laughter: Expressions of Emotions in the Middle Ages*, edited by P. Fönegård et al., 182–92. Konferenser 92. Stockholm: Kungl, 2017.
Aquinas, St. Thomas. *Summa Theologica*. London: Burnes, Oates, and Washbourne, 1923.
Arendt, Hannah. *The Life of the Mind*. Vol. 1, *Thinking*. New York: Harcourt, Brace, Javanovich, 1971.
Ascombe, G. E. M. *Wittgenstein: Philosophical Investigations*. New York: Macmillan, 1963.
Barnes, Julian. *Elizabeth Finch*. New York: Knopf, 2022.
Bonner, Gerald. "Augustine and Mysticism." In *Augustine: Mystic and Mystagogue*, edited by Frederick Van Fleteren et al., 113–57. New York: Peter Lang, 1994.
———. "Libido and Concupiscentia in St. Augustine." In *God's Decree and Man's Destiny*, by Gerald Bonner, 303–14. Variorum Collected Studies Series 255. London: Variorum, 1987.
Brown, Peter. *Augustine of Hippo*. 2nd ed. Berkeley: University of California Press, 2000.
Burnaby, John. *Amor Dei: A Study of the Religion of St. Augustine*. Eugene, OR: Wipf and Stock, 2007.
Burns, J. Patout, Jr. "Human Agency in Augustine's Doctrine of Predestination and Perseverance." *Augustinian Studies* 48 (1977) 45–71.
Cameron, Michael. "*Totus Christus* and the Psychagogy of Augustine's Sermons." *Augustinian Studies* 36.1 (2005) 59–70.
Canning, Raymond. *Instructing Beginners in the Faith*. The Augustine Series 5. New York: New City Press, 2006.
Carruthers, Mary. *The Book of Memory: A Study of Memory in Medieval Culture*. Cambridge Studies in Medieval Literature 70. New York: Cambridge University Press, 1990.

Bibliography

———. *The Craft of Thought: Meditation, Rhetoric, and the Making of Images, 400–1200*. Cambridge Studies in Medieval Literature 34. New York: Cambridge University Press, 1998.

Cary, Phillip. *Augustine's Invention of the Inner Self: The Legacy of a Christian Platonist*. New York: Oxford University Press, 2000.

Cavadini, John C. "Reconsidering Augustine on Marriage and Concupiscence." *Augustinian Studies* 48.2 (2017) 183–99.

Clemens, Thomas. "Augustine and Porphyry." Augustinian Institute, Villanova University Conference, Zoom, May 4, 2021.

Collingwood, R. G. *The Idea of History*. London: Clarendon, 1946.

Conybeare, Catherine. *The Irrational Augustine*. New York: Oxford University Press, 2006.

Couenhoven, Jesse. "St. Augustine's Doctrine of Original Sin." *Augustinian Studies* 36.2 (2005) 45–71.

Damasio, Antonio. *Feeling and Knowing: Making Minds Conscious*. New York: Pantheon, 2021.

Davidson, Arnold. *The Emergence of Sexuality: Historical Epistemology and the Formation of Concepts*. Cambridge: Harvard University Press, 2001.

Descartes, René. *Meditations on First Philosophy*. Great Books of the Western World 31. Chicago: Encyclopedia Britannica, 1952.

Dupont, Anthony, Wim François, and Johan Leemans, eds. *Nos sumus Tempora: Studies on Augustine and his Reception Offered to Mathijs Lamberigts*. Leuven: Peters, 2020.

Fleteren, Frederick van, et al. eds. *Augustine: Mystic and Mystagogue*. New York: Peter Lang, 1994.

———. "Editorial Conclusions." In *Augustine: Mystic and Mystagogue*, 547–53. New York: Peter Lang, 1994.

Foucault, Michel. *Confessions of the Flesh*. Vol 4. Translated by Robert Hurley. New York: Pantheon, 2021.

Freud, Sigmund. *New Introductory Lectures*. Edited by James Strachey. New York: W. W. Norton, 1965.

Gilson, Étienne. *The Christian Philosophy of St. Augustine*. New York: Random House, 1960.

Greenblatt, Stephen. "The Invention of Sex." *The New Yorker*, June 19, 2017. https://www.newyorker.com/magazine/2017/06/19/how-st-augustine-invented-sex.

Grote, Andreas E. J., and Christof Müller. "Augustinus, Epistula 263 an Sapida: Systematische Darstellung, Einzelkommentiurung, Übersetzung." In *Nos sumus Tempora: Studies on Augustine and his Reception Offered to Mathijs Lamberigts*, edited by Anthony Dupont, Wim François, and Johan Leemans, 113–42. Leuven: Peters, 2020.

Grove, Kevin G. *Augustine on Memory*. New York: Oxford University Press, 2021.

Haraway, Donna, et al. *Writing on the Body: Embodiment and Feminist Theory*. New York: State University of New York Press, 1997.

Bibliography

Harrison, Carol. *The Art of Listening in the Early Church.* Oxford: Oxford University Press, 2013.

Hockenbery, Jennifer. "The He, She, and It of God: Translating St. Augustine's Gendered Latin into English." *Augustinian Studies* 36.2 (2005) 433–44.

Jones, A. H. M. *The Later Roman Empire.* Vol. 2. Oxford: Blackwell, 1964.

Kennedy, Robert P. "*The Irrational Augustine* (Book Review)." *Augustinian Studies* 39.1 (2008) 131–34.

Lawless, George, OSA. *Augustine of Hippo and His Monastic Rule.* New York: Oxford, 1987.

Marion, Jean Luc. *In the Self's Place: The Approach of Augustine.* Translated by Jeffrey L. Kosky. Stanford University Press, 2021.

Meer, Frederick, Van der. *Augustine the Bishop.* London: Sheed and Ward, 1961.

Miles, Margaret R. "Augustine and Freud: The Secularization of Self-Deception." In *Augustine and Psychology*, edited by K. Paffenroth, R. Kennedy, and J. Doody, 115–30. Lanham, MD: Lexington, 2012.

———. *Augustine on the Body.* Missoula: Scholars Press, 1979; reprinted Eugene, OR: Cascade, 2009.

———. *Beyond the Centaur: Imagining the Intelligent Body.* Eugene, OR: Cascade, 2014.

———. *Reading Augustine on Memory, Marriage, Tears, and Meditation.* London: Bloomsbury Academic, 2021.

———. *Recollections and Reconsiderations.* Eugene, OR: Cascade, 2018.

———. "Sex and the City (of God): Is Sex Forfeited or Fulfilled in Augustine's Resurrection of Body?" *Journal of the American Academy of Religion* 73.2 (June 2005) 307–27.

Mohrmann, Christine. "Saint Augustin écrivain." *Recherches Augustiniennes* 1 (1958) 43–66.

Nagy, Piroska. "The Power of Medieval Emotions and Change." In *Tears, Sighs, and Laughter: Expressions of Emotions in the Middle Ages*, edited by P. Fönegård et al., 13–40. Konferenser 92. Stockholm: Kungel, 2017.

O'Connell, R. J. *St. Augustine's Early Theory of Man.* Cambridge: Harvard University Press, 1968.

O'Donnell, James J. *Augustine: A New Biography.* New York: HarperCollins, 2005.

———. *Augustine, Sinner and Saint.* London: Profile, 2005.

———. "The Next Life of St. Augustine." In *The Limits of Christianity*, edited by William Klingshirn and Mark Vessey, 215–31. Ann Arbor: University of Michigan Press, 1999.

O'Meara, John J. *Porphyry's Philosophy from Oracles.* Paris: Études Augustiniennes, 1959.

Pascal, Blaise. *Pensées.* Translated by A. J. Krailsheimer. Baltimore: Penguin, 1966.

Possidius. *Sancti Augustinus Uita*, Life of St. Augustine. Translated by Herbert Weiskotten. Merchantville, NJ: Evolution, 2008.

Rapp, Claudia. *Holy Bishops in Late Antiquity: The Nature of Christian Leadership in an Age of Transition.* Berkeley: University of California Press, 2005.

Bibliography

Robinson, J. A. T. *The Body: A Study in Pauline Theology*. London: SCM, 1952.

Roessli, Jean-Michel. "Mirabilia, miraculum." In *Augustinus Lexikon* vol. 4, fasc. 1/2, edited by Robert Dodaro et al., 25–29. Basel: Schwabe, 2012.

Sanlon, Peter T. *Augustine's Theology of Preaching*. Minneapolis: Fortress, 2014.

Shanzer, Danuta. "Augustine's Anonyma I and Cornelius's Concubines." *Augustinian Studies* 48.2 (2017) 201–24.

Sheets Johnstone, Maxine. *The Corporeal Turn: An Interdisciplinary Reader*. Exeter: Imprint Academic, 2009.

Simon, Bill. *Postmodern Sexualities*. New York: Routledge, 1996.

Stock, Brian. *St. Augustine's Inner Dialogue: The Soliloquy in Late Antiquity*. New York: Cambridge University Press, 2010.

Strachey, James, ed. *Sigmund Freud: New Introductory Lectures*. New York: W. W. Norton, 1965.

Teske, Roland J. "St. Augustine and the Vision of God." In *Augustine: Mystic and Mystagogue*, edited by Frederick Van Fleteren et al., 287–308. New York: Peter Lang, 1994.

Ticciati, S. *A New Apophaticism: Augustine and the Redemption of Signs*. Leiden: Brill, 2015.

Tonna-Barthet, Antonio. "Augustinian Mystical Theology." In *Augustine: Mystic and Mystagogue*, edited by Frederick Van Fleteren et al., 555–86. New York: Peter Lang, 1994.

Traherne, Thomas. *Centuries of Meditation*. London: Dobell, 1908.

Wilken, Thomas. "Cyril of Alexandria's *Contra Iulianum*." In *The Limits of Ancient Christianity*, edited by William E. Klingshirn and Mark Vessey, 42–60. Ann Arbor: University of Michigan Press, 1999.

Williams, Norman P. *Ideas of the Fall and of Original Sin*. New York: Longmans Green, 1927.

Wittgenstein, Ludwig. *Philosophical Investigations*. Translated by G. E. M. Ascombe. New York: Macmillan, 1963.

———. *Tractatus Logico Philosophicus*. Translated by D. F. Pears and B. F. McGuinnes. London: Blackwell, 1961.

Index

abstraction ("leave it to God"), xxv, 19, 35
   inscrutable doctrines, 35, 111
Adeodatus, Augustine's son, 26
ageism (in translations of Augustine), xxv, xviii, 20, 61n29, 56, 74–76, 106
Anthony, St., 34
Augustine of Hippo, St.
   age, xvii
      youth, 81–83, 33, 46, *Confessions*, 46, 78–82
      mid-life, 1–2, Cassiciacum, 25–28, early theology of resurrection, 100–101; baptism, 6
      old, xxv, 2, 16–17, 20–21, 29–32, 46, 75–78, 83, 103; *Retractationes*, 85
   bishop, 17, 98; bishop and monk, 20–22
   "by himself," 77, 86–89, "in myself," 42, privacy, 21, 23, 77, 86
   conversions (Augustine), 47, 80, 82
   celibacy (conversion to), 34, 57–59
   death, xx, 41, 73, 77–78, 89–90, 96, a "teachable moment," 78
   experience, 3, 5, 17, 29, 35–36, 39–45, 59, 62, 69, 79; conversion to celibacy, 41, 80–81
   knowledge (of God), 42, self knowledge (Augustine), 35, 92
   leisure, *otium*, 21, 26
   limitations, xxv, 9–10, of experience, 107
   memory (*see* meditation, memory)
   as pastor, 104–6, 108–9 (*see* sermons)
   Retractationes, 74–75, 78, 83–84
   self identity, xix, 47
authority, 6–7, 19–20

baptism, 6
beauty, *On the Beautiful and the Fitting*, xxi
   delight, xxiv, 63, 68
   feeling, 91, 103–4n23
   God (as beauty), 44, 80, 94–95
   linking present to resurrected bodies, 103, 109–10
   nature, xxi, 80, 101–2

Index

belief, 6–8, 20
    difficulty of, xix, 8–9, 107, 110
    reasonable, 6
    and knowledge, xxiii, 7, 29
    and understanding, 9
    and practice, 48, 52
binaries, 58, 64, 73
body of Christ, 8
    "becoming Christ," 48–49, 72
    individual and corporate, 105, 112
body, human (*nunc*), x, xvii, 7, 8–10, 36, 91, 94–95, 104–5, 110
    Jesus' human body, 36, 60,
    flesh, 36, 91, 104–5, 110–11
    and humility, 16
    (*tunc*), 94, 97, 104–5
    Resurrection painting, Signorelli, ix–xi
    Augustine's early understanding, 100–102 (*see also* resurrection)
Brown, Peter, *Augustine of* Hippo, 76

Carruthers, Mary, *Craft of Thought*, 87–88
Cassiciacum, 25–28
Church, Christian
    Body of Christ, xx, xxvi, 10, 48, 71–72, 99, 105,
    "becoming Christ," 16, 48, 52, 71
    image of Christ, 48
    Jesus' miracles as establishing the Church, 7
    Church as M/mother, breasts, 6; milk, 26, 47, 102–3
    doctrine, xix, xx, implied by Church practices, 65
    original sin, 36–38, 54, 71
    physicality of, 38, 72
    infant baptism, 65

predestination, perseverance, xx, 35, 51–52
    and feeling, 35–36
    and fear, 54, 64–65
    preaching predestination, 51–52, 65–69
    grace, 36, 67–68, and free will, 36, 67–68
    importance of doctrines for the present, 51, 65, 100, 111
    and practice, 51, 65
    controversy, 18, 20
Cicero, 3, 25, 84
confession as praise, 82, 110
    Confessions, 71, 77–79, 82, 96
    as penitance, xx, 77–78, 90

Davidson, Arnold, *Emergence of Sexuality*, discursive fields, 24–25
death, and fear, 94
    and love, 73
Descartes, 3, 56
desire, 40–43, 46–47, 69, 105, and delight, xxiv, 63, 68, 100

ear (inner), xxii, 10, 32n59, 35, 40–43, 62, 66–67 (*see also* preaching predestination)
eyes, ix, 10, 40, 85, 93–94, 108–9

fear, 31, 64, 70–73, 93–94
    blocks pride, 91–94
    and love, 31, 94
feeling, xxii, 3–4, 17, 23, 33–36, 53, 56–59
    "deepest human feeling," 112
    and thinking, 3, 42, 55, 57
    and humility, 55, 59
    and understanding, 6–8
    and doctrine, 35
    see also tears

Index

fire, xxvii, 39

Grove, Kevin G., *Augustine on Memory*, xxiv, 47–48
   "first order theology," 61–62
   body of Christ, 47–48

Harrison, Carol, *The Art of Listening in the Early Church*, xxvi, 9, 63
Hippo, 29–30 (*see also* sermons)
hope, 69, 98, 109
humility, xxiii, xxv, 16, 31–32, and *passim*
   Jesus embodiment of, 35–36, 49–50, 59–61, 73, 76
   and love, 32
   and pride, 35, 59–61

intus (inner), 16, 34, 41–42, 68

Julian of Eclanum, xx, xxiii, 9, 20, 35, 38–39, 51–52, 64–65, 75–76

knowledge, 6–7, 29–30

language, 63, 64n41
learning, xviii, 3, 59, 73
life, God as, xxiv, 44–45, 70, 102, 111
love, xx, xxiii–xxiv, 24
   "a stronger form of will," 30–33, 73
   absorbs fear and lust, 31
   God as, xxiv, 42–44, 52, 72
   as beauty, 4, 2
   of neighbor, xxvi, 43, 105–6
   of self, 29
   guardian of humility, 32
lust, xxi, 27, 31–32, 36–37, 69

Manichaean theology, 5
marriage, 27, 47

meditation, xix, 18–19, 21–23, 25
memory, 23, 39–43, 79, 86–89, 94, 101–3
   influenced by rhetoric, 87–88, 94
   steps, 91–93
   Confessions as, 47
   feeling, tears, 4–6, 41, 74, 81–82, 87–88, 90–91, 94
   and beauty, 91, 94
   and fear, 91, 93
   fire, 23, 39
method
   in *Beautiful Bodies*, xv, xviii;
   discursive fields, 24–25
   contemporary interpretation, xv, "silent thoughts," 55–56
   proof texts, xxviii
miracles, xviii–xix, 1–17
   contemporary, assisting belief 10–11
   human birth, human beings, 13, 109–10
   ordinary, 11–14, extraordinary, 14–15, inner, 15–16
Monica, 26–27
monasteries, 22
mortality, 107–9, 112

O'Donnell, James, 85

penitence, 83, 74, 77, 90
pilgrimage as metaphor, 50–51
Plato, Platonic tradition, xvii, xix, 26, 28, 98, 103
   Porphyry, 97–98
   beauty, and Plotinus, 78, 103–4n23
Possidius, xxi, xxiii, 21, 49, 77, 90
preaching, xxii, 49, 61–63
   and rhetoric, 84–85
   and feeling, 63
   preaching predestination, 65–69; "leave it to God," 73, 103, 108

Index

psalms, xix, 47, 50, 90, 99

reason, rationality, 6–7, 56
  reasonable belief, 6, 56
  see also Cassiciacum
resurrection, resurrection body, 104–6
  early theology of, 100–103
  late, feeling, 103
  beauty as link, 104, 107, 110
  "fully alive," 104
rhetoric, x, 7, 9–10, 49, 56–57, 83–84, 87, 90

scripture, xviii, 29–30, 34, 49, 64, 83, 85
  Augustine's most-often quoted (1 Cor 13:12), 69
  and experience, 29–30

sermons (Augustine), xxv–xxvi, 8–10, 20, 24, 34, 49–50, 61–63, 99, 105, 112
Signorelli, Luca, ix–x
"silent thoughts," Foucault, xxv, 29–30, 55
sin, 79

tears, in meditation, 71–74, 81, 87–88

Vandals, xx, 76
virginity, 32
vision (of God), xxiii, 43–44, *id quod est*, 70–72

will, 32, 36, 58 (*see also* love)
wisdom, xvii, 42, 84